MAXIMUM LIVING

IN A PRESSURE-COOKER WORLD

MAXIMUM LIVING IN A PRESSURE-COOKER WORLD

Tim Timmons

Research and Editorial Assistance
by Martha Greene

WORD BOOKS
PUBLISHER
WACO, TEXAS

To my three little "thinkers":

Tammy

Tacy

Timothy

Acknowledgments:

Thanks to:

Dr. Daniel J. Vanian, Ph.D.

Dr. E. James Stanley, M.D.

for helpful interaction on the concept of the "mental checkup."

Thanks to:

Judy Wilson

for the extra hours in typing and preparing the manuscript for publication.

CONTENTS

Humpty Dumpty sat on a wall,
Humpty Dumpty had a great fall,
All the king's horses
And all the king's men
Couldn't put Humpty Dumpty together again.
                          Humpty Dumpty

PREFACE:

Humpty Dumpty Was Pushed!

HAVE YOU EVER FELT like Humpty Dumpty—pushed and pressured to pieces? Unlike Humpty Dumpty, who even with the help of all the king's horses and all the king's men couldn't get himself back together, most people can get themselves back together again. But they climb back on their walls only to be pushed off all over again! After a few more pushes knock you off various walls, you discover very quickly that it becomes increasingly more difficult to pull yourself together again. But why so many falls off so many walls? It's your *perspective*—or your lack of it!

A full perspective forces you to ask pertinent questions about your pleasures (sitting on walls) and your predicaments (falling off walls). Why do I like sitting on walls? Who pushed me? Why was I pushed? Why do I fall when I'm pushed? Why do I break into pieces when I fall? Why do I feel I've lost another piece every time I try to put myself back together again? As you begin to answer these perspective questions you are launched into a new life style—that of knowing about yourself and taking control of what you know. You can begin *to act* rather than *to react*—to live life

9

by your choice rather than by your circumstances or the choice of others!

Most people are suffering from a faulty perspective. There are at least three types of faulty perspectives. The first is a *passive perspective.* Here you may understand all there is to know about walls, pushes, and falls and be committed to what you know, but you aren't personally involved in your commitment. In other words you are committed to what you should do theoretically, but you aren't practicing it. You aren't following through. You're like the Kamikaze pilot who flew thirty-three missions!

The second type of faulty perspective is a *partial perspective.* Here you have a limited knowledge about walls, pushes, and falls. You just do not see the whole picture, and consequently, you lack an adequate basis for action. I experience this constantly when I counsel with couples. Almost every time I see the husband and wife separately, I get a faulty perspective on their marital situation. After I've listened to the wife, I'm convinced she's married to the "No. 1 Clod of the Year!" Then her husband walks in and as I listen to his side of the story, I become convinced he should be given a medal for hanging in there! Until I can move to a fuller perspective my partial perspective paralyzes me from acting wisely!

The third type of faulty perspective is a *prejudiced perspective.* Through this perspective lens you view the walls, pushes, and falls the way you want to view them, in spite of every evidence to the contrary! Many people absolutely refuse to acknowledge evidence, as this scenario so clearly and cleverly illustrates:

Once upon a time there was a man who thought he was dead. His concerned wife and friends sent him to the friendly neighborhood psychiatrist. The psychiatrist determined to cure him by convincing him of one fact that contradicted his belief that he was dead. The psychiatrist decided to use the simple truth that dead men do not bleed. He put his patient to work reading medical texts, observing autopsies, and so on.

After weeks of effort, the patient finally said, "All right, all right! You've convinced me! Dead men do not bleed." Whereupon the psychiatrist stuck him in the arm with a needle, and the blood flowed. The man looked down with a contorted, ashen face and cried: "Good Lord! Dead men do bleed after all!"[1]

Since a faulty perspective—passive or partial or prejudiced—is so common, then how do you cultivate a full and balanced perspective on life's pleasures and predicaments? The answer is simple, yet surprising. *Think!*

It's estimated that only 5 percent of the world think, 15 percent think they think, and 80 percent would rather die than think! An educational study showed that when people are presented with a new concept: 50 percent go along with it and 30 percent don't, both without thinking or evaluating, 15 percent take longer to make a decision but still without thinking or evaluating, and 5 percent truly think and evaluate before making a decision.

Sales industries consistently find that approximately 5 percent of their salespeople rise to the top and are responsible for the majority of their productivity. It's also interesting to note that when faced with sickness, a tragedy or a crisis of some sort, only 5 percent will come through it all a better person. The other 95 percent will come out worse for the experience!

A 5 percenter—a thinker! Thinking is the process of expanding your perspective on life. It's the art of viewing the whole wall without finding yourself in midair! As you expand your perspective, you may discover that you have several (not just one) options as to where you sit (not on walls)—or stand. You may also discover that you don't want to sit on walls anymore!

With a faulty perspective, life (people and circumstances) controls you, but with a full perspective you can take control of life. Instead of feeling like Humpty Dumpty, always getting pushed and pressured to pieces, you can make things happen on purpose—positive things! A full perspective will help you live life with more confidence in yourself, compassion for others, and commitment to the future.

Something that will guide your thinking toward a full perspective on life is a mental checkup. We are diligent to recommend that everyone have a *physical*, periodically. Since most physical problems relate directly to a mental (psychological, emotional, spiritual, and so on) source, then why not a *mental?*

I do need to issue one warning at this point: *A mental checkup will not work unless you are willing to think!* If you're not willing to risk burning out a fuse or two in your head, then turn your thinking cap in right now and try to get your money back on this book. The first thing you must force yourself to think about is your own person. This is the most difficult level on which to develop a full perspective. Second, you must force yourself to think about others. It's easy to call it depression when it's my problem but recession when it's someone else's. Third, you must force yourself to think about future generations. What you do or don't do with your life will be extremely significant for those who follow you.

I speak from personal experience when I say you will never be the same after reading this book. It has made a tremendous impact on me and I don't ever expect to shake its effect. If you're a 5 percenter, the mental checkup will help you successfully get through the piles of life. But if you're a 95 percenter and choose to remain there, the piles of life will overwhelm you and eventually smother you. Only 5 percent think, 15 percent think they think, and 80 percent would rather die than think! What about you?

INTRODUCTION:
Mental Checkup or Check-out?

Dear Ann Landers:

I don't care what you do with this letter. You don't even have to read it if you don't want to, but I have to write it. A lot of people wonder why anyone would want to commit suicide. Most of us have a decent life and so it seems like a crazy thing to do. But it doesn't seem so crazy to me. I'm a guy who wishes he didn't have to get up every morning and face the day. I'm 17 years old and a junior in high school. I'm empty, useless, and tired of struggling. I feel like I'm in everybody's way, and I don't think anybody would give a damn if I disappeared from the face of the earth. I have no idea why I was ever born. I don't fit in any place.

I know you can't do anything about all this, but I wanted to explain to somebody what goes through a person's mind before he pulls the trigger or swallows one too many pills.

Signed,
A nonperson!

Another nonperson checking out! Each year tens of thousands of people choose to check out through suicide. (The highest rate of suicidal check-out is now found in two unlikely groups—the medical profession and teenagers.) But suicide is not the only check-out which is on the increase. There is another kind of check-out which is engulfing more and more people in our world. It's a *living* check-out, and it has pene-

13

trated every level of society. It occurs when a person dies, but isn't ready for burial yet! His tombstone epithet might read: "Died at 33, buried at 65!" It's when a person becomes a nonperson—when he checks out mentally.

Personness

To check out mentally is to experience a miserable existence. Instead of *living* as a unique, creative person, you begin *existing* as a nonperson. Personness involves meaningful actions, choices, reasons, values, responsibility, and purposes. Without these personness characteristics you become at best a higher animal or machine, but never a healthy person. A nonperson suffers from *dissatisfaction* with himself, his relationships, and his future. This in turn produces *apathy* (not caring about anyone or anything else) and *destination sickness* (lacking a sense of destiny and hope).

These three common diseases (dissatisfaction, apathy, and destination sickness) infect presidents and paupers, rich and poor, white collar workers and blue collar workers, marrieds and singles, male and female, adults and children. No one is immune from catching these deadening diseases. There is the woman who finds herself in the pressurized position of running the household and family. As she reacts against the doormat syndrome and gropes for her identity and self-worth she asks, "Is this all there is to life?" Then there is the university student who feels the insignificance of being just another number or the insecurity of an uncertain future. There is also the successful executive who decides he has given enough of his life to being a good husband and father and must now do something for himself. And there is the single parent who faces the pressure of being both mom and dad to the children, and the one all alone in the crowd wondering if anyone cares.

If you are alive and living in the same world as I am, you know that the above illustrations aren't just theoretical. They're all too real! I see these same problems intensified and multiplied every day as I counsel, and as I lecture throughout the world. It's one thing to talk about nameless cases, but when you are suffering from one or more of these diseases, it becomes a heartrending experience. It's real. And it's spreading in epidemic proportions!

Mental Checkup!

Instead of joining the massive check-out, we must encourage one another to have a *mental checkup!* A mental checkup is the process of developing a healthy you—your personness. It's learning to fight the diseases of dissatisfaction, apathy, and destination sickness. It's a personal struggle for your own life and the lives of your loved ones. A mental checkup is a search for answers to the most fundamental personness questions: *Why am I? Who am I? Where am I going?* To ignore these questions is to commit mental suicide—the death of your personness. Everyone has to make a choice—*a mental checkup or check-out!*

Feet Firmly Planted in Midair!

Our modern world is an exhilarating place to live. We know more, we can do more, and we have more than any other society in the history of mankind. Just plug it in, push the button, and you have instant—everything! But along with having everything *in* an instant, we only seem to have it *for* an instant—everything is happening at such a breathless pace! The world is passing us by so fast that it becomes nearly impossible for a person to get his/her head together long enough to consider: Why am I? Who am I? Where am I going? No one—not even the most brilliant scientist alive today—really knows where science is taking us. We are aboard a train which is gathering speed, racing down a track on which there are an unknown number of switches leading to unknown destinations. No single scientist is in the engine cab and there may be demons at the switches. Most of society is in the caboose looking backward.[1] Everything is out of control. It's like having your feet firmly planted in midair!

Time Bombs!

So what is the underlying problem? Why is it so easy to mentally check out and so difficult to mentally check up?

15

I think it's because of the time bombs (explosive issues that affect our personness) that are constantly going off in our society and leaving a pile of psychological wreckage inside people. The debris of the various time bombs is devastating, and every waking moment lights another fuse with the matchsticks of TV, radio, newspapers, books, magazines, people, and so on.

In the first part of this book we will examine ten of the most destructive time bombs and expose their interlocking effects:

1. The Ecological Time Bomb

There are more than four billion people in the world today, and at the present growth rate of 1.85 percent annually this number will double in about 38 years. Apocalyptic warnings about this potential population bomb have been around since the late sixties, and although it is doubtful whether the explosion has occurred, the problem is still present. Zero population growth enthusiasts have done much to delay detonation, yet the message and the means are still unknown to many of the underdeveloped countries, and the developed countries continue to extend man's three score and ten years through medical and technical advancements. The *demand* increases—for food, housing, jobs, and consumer goods and services, and the *drain* decreases—available land, fresh water, and energy. The competition for the demanded and draining life substances fosters not only the external ills of pollution, but also the external ills of personness. *Will the little old woman in the shoe be able to contain her children, or will she soon be found stepping on her own laces and left with her tongue hanging out?*

2. The Chemical Time Bomb

The greater the crowd the greater the contamination, and the accumulating masses of people are stamping "Mess" indelibly on the environment. The quality of life has continued to fall. Nothing is immune—from the breath of death in Los Angeles, to the septic tank of Lake Erie, to the paved plant species of Florida and the tree-plucked island of Java, to the evicted Bengal tigers of the Indian subcontinent. The air, the water, the soil and those that grow in it and roam upon it, all bear the earmarks of an ailing environment. Unfortunately, because man must breathe the air, drink the water, and gather sustenance from the soil, no one is immune. Fortunately, most of the ugly environmental earmarks are man-made, and therefore are controllable, and/or changeable. It is possible to restore a healthy relationship between the biological, chemical, and physical systems. However, it is also possible that man will choose not to. The earth is sickened with the wastes and chemicals of man and yet his existence depends upon it. *We are what we breathe . . . and drink . . . and eat . . . . What shall it be? What shall we become?*

3. THE BIOLOGICAL TIME BOMB

The cradle of life and the grave of death have long been matters confined to the discussion of philosophers and the description of poets. The first breath and the last resided under the supreme reign of Nature, and each man existed and expired under her rule. Now a new creature has entered her courts, one who questions her right to rule and seeks to control the extending and extinguishing of her hand. Man has always had the means of averting the hand of Nature, crude though they were: rhythm was practiced, semen was spilled, infanticide was practiced, the ailing were killed, and the old were left to die. We have sophisticated those practices with contraceptives, abortion, and euthanasia, but moving away from or out from under her hand is a lot different from controlling it. The new creature has a new term—genetic engineering—and a new challenge—to create man, physically, mentally, and emotionally, according to designed specifications. An awesome power. An overwhelming potential. *Who will be left to live happily ever after—beauty or the beast?*

4. THE PSYCHOLOGICAL TIME BOMB

The physical form of the universe and its inhabitants are not sufficient to content the supreme creature, man. With one

17

hand caressing and shaping the visible, he turns his other hand to reach for the invisible—the metaphysical—the mind and the spirit. It took man a long time to put "ology" behind his "Psyche" and begin to view his mind as the center of thought, feeling, and behavior—consciously or unconsciously relating the body to his physical and social environment. But once he had the questions as to *how* it does so and the answers as to *why* it does so the way it does so becomes endless.

It is said that the great French philosopher, Sartre, summed up all of life with the statement, "To be is to do!" Camus, his contemporary, summed up all of life with a conflicting statement, "To do is to be!" Then Frank Sinatra came along and put them both together in a song—"Do-be-do-be-do!" In a sense, that's the best summary of the psychological time bomb. When you're bombarded by all the varied and mutually conflicting psychological therapies (Behavior, Gestalt, Psychoanalysis, and so on) and psychological experiences (EST, Lifespring, and so on), you can easily come away saying, "Do-be-do-be-do!"

Look within, those who have embraced "Psyche" shout. *"It's all in your head!" But the shouts are so many and so loud . . . which is correct . . . which works? Which do doctors recommend most for relating things in your head?*

5. The Parapsychological Time Bomb

"Mirror, mirror on the wall, tell me that this isn't all!" Somewhere beyond man's head, yet beneath the heavens, is another area of the invisible—a "Twilight Zone" of "between" phenomena, not explainable by known natural laws, yet experienced in the known natural universe. Certain people can perceive things out of the range of human sense—*clairvoyance;* know things in advance of their occurrence—*precognition;* communicate by exercising a sixth sense—*telepathy;* and move inanimate and remote objects with an unseen arm—*psychokenesis.*

What is this intangible image produced in the mirror, this psychic power attributed to certain individuals? Is it simply the conscious exercise of a preciously unconscious ability, or is it an unconscious ability provided by an outside source? Those involved with *ESP* (Extra Sensory Perception) and *PK* (Psychokinesis) would emphatically put it in the former category, while those involved with *astrology, spiritualism,* and *witchcraft* ascribe it to the latter. *Astrology* employs the heavenly bodies with their positions and aspects to predict the course of human affairs, and the charting of such has become a science and art of its own. *Spiritualism* employs some sort of medium (spirit, ouija board, tarot cards, UFO's, and so on) and through various methods (fortune telling, seances, necromancy, automatic writing, rappings, table turnings, and so on) receives messages. *Witchcraft* employs the devil or some other "good spirit" to exert influence, attract or charm (magic, sorcery, voodoo).

The unexplainable and bizarre beyond—the "Twilight Zone" between man's head and the heavens. "Mirror, mirror on the wall, tell me what to make of it all!"

6. THE RELIGIOUS TIME BOMB

"Oh, East is East, and West is West, and never the twain shall meet . . ." voiced Kipling with confidence, for there was no possible way they possibly could. Though they still might be said to stand at the "ends of the earth," the gap between the East and the West has narrowed to such an extent that the superlative in Rudyard's ballad is no longer valid. When man turns his gaze on the invisible from within to without he has, not a distinctly separated spectrum to choose from, but an amalgamation of answers as to an "other" in the universe. The major religions of the world have joined hands forming a paper doll chain of outstretched arms and smiling faces, each seeking to solicit followers into its fold.

The "other," that which is outside man's own head in the realm of the supernatural, is called by various names and described with varying characteristics. It is packaged as Thetan, Perfect Knowledge, Krishna, God, or Jesus Christ. It is presented under the auspices of *missions*—Scientology and Divine Light; *mystics*—Krishna Consciousness and Zen; *families*—Children of God and Love Israel; *churches*—Local and Unification; and man-made religious systems—Catholic, Protestant and Jewish. It is promoted first by founders and leaders and then by their followers. They promise "spiritual awareness" leading to a more fruitful, happy life, a "blissed-out" existence of perfect peace, "altered-consciousness" to expel the directed thoughts of the external world, "the way" to God establishing communication with God, existing with him, or acquiring his essence.

If there is some "other" outside of man which holds the answer to his humanity and his happiness, are there people who truly understand it, and are there groups who accurately expound it? Heaven help us get on the right "twain"!

7. The Educational Time Bomb

The morning paper hits the front door long before our feet hit the floor, a click of the radio accompanies us to and from work in our car, billboards and store signs spice up the scenery, magazines cover our coffee tables, the 6 o'clock news entertains the evening meal, and best sellers and academy award winners fill up our free time. All of this is in addition to the twelve to twenty years spent studying for a degree and the endless extension classes taken after the diploma.

Whether formally or informally, the bombardment of information is a continuous explosion, as to its effect, both of the knowledge acquired and the behavior produced. TV is the primary educator outside the classroom (for each household it has an average "on-time" of 6 hours and 7 minutes per day), with newspapers, magazines, and radio ranking below it respectively. We know more, about more people, places, and things than ever before, and· this information is becoming available to increasing numbers of people. (As well as becoming a little overwhelming!)

The institutionalized information—formal education—has been shifting to gear itself and its students to this increasing and ever changing information. "Inquiry"; "Problem Solving"; "Sensitivity Training"; "Operant Conditioning" and "Unfreezing" have been incorporated into elementary and secondary

20

curriculum placing the school in the position of both educator and "clinic."

Along with changes in the "ways" of teaching has come a change in the "whats," with less emphasis on the knowledge imparted and more on the behavior produced. Perhaps there is an increased ability to adapt—yet there also seems to be an increasing opposition: student walkouts, protests, riots, vandalism, assaults on teachers and teacher strikes.

What kind of information is being disseminated, and what kind of behavior is being produced? What kind of control is being maintained (if any)? Where are Dick and Jane headed?

8. The Political Time Bomb

". . . with liberty and justice for all" has been pledged for over 200 years, and throughout that time the government has been its guardian. "Of the people, by the people and for the people" has been structuring the social system and acting as the authority to insure those rights. In colonial days the job was relatively easy, the body to be governed was small, and their way of life simple. In postindustrial days the job is increasingly difficult, the body to be governed is large, and their way of life complex. The 39 men who banded together to sign the Constitution have multiplied into a bureaucracy of over 14 million now employed to operate the areas of the body politic.

The value of the politic is most often weighed in that of the dollar—what will it buy and more importantly what is it worth? There is more money and more credit but also more inflation. Incomes increase but so do prices and taxes. For those who can't make their budgets balance (a practice from which the Federal Government has been excused) there are endless open-ended programs available to care for them. Others take the matter into their own hands and directly into the pockets of others.

Unfortunately this explosion can't be confined to our shores. It has been felt on a global scale and so also involves the issues of foreign policy and military strength, foreign relations

21

and aid, human rights, detente, arms limitation and nuclear warfare.

The government is making more and more decisions covering and controlling more and more areas. *What is the policy ". . . for which it stands"? Are the people or the politicians determining its destiny?*

9. THE SOCIOLOGICAL TIME BOMB

Along with the remarkably rapid development and advancement of man has come a change in his social relationships, in the structure of society. With urban concentration and mass communication he has been forced to relate, not only on an individual level, but also on a societal level. The problems he faces and the decisions he must make involve not only himself but society as a whole. Societal decisions have become necessary—population, pollution, genetic engineering, education, urban renewal, and medical care—as has an ordering unit to make them. (The politic's purpose.)

The basic unit of society used to be the individual, and the primary purpose of society was to allow the individual to fulfill himself (expecting that everyone would differ in their abilities and achievements, but would be given equal opportunity). The basic unit now *is* society, and its primary purpose is to allow society to fulfill itself (expecting that everyone will have results, despite differing abilities and achievements). What are the values (What is right?) and goals (What is good?) of this new unit, and how can it best accomplish its purpose? (What's the plan?) What kind of requirements and restrictions are to be placed on the individual, groups, minorities, or nations in the intrest of the "family of man"? (The politic's power!)

There are also some pressing questions, and some staggering statistics, concerning "man's family." The altar and the attorney's office are now doing an equal amount of business, with fewer and fewer steps between the courtship and the courtroom. Many couples do seek the help of counselors to avoid divorce, but many more can face neither court nor counselor and simply resign themselves to a miserable marital existence. The highest cost of the broken relationships is paid by the children—used, abused, and tossed between mom and dad.

Relationships—societal, marital, parent-child—the "family of man" and man's family. "As the World Turns," what will happen in the next episode?

10. THE PHILOSOPHICAL TIME BOMB

Most people would not consider themselves philosophers in the *classical* sense of the word: a student of the academic subject, exercising the discipline in the areas of logic, ethics, aesthetics, metaphysics, and epistemology. However, all people (whether they consider themselves to be or not) are philosophers in the *casual* sense of the word: one having a world view—a basic set of values by which to live, to define and deal with reality—seeking answers to the basic questions in life. In turn, all people (whether they realize it or not) decide the direction and destiny both of themselves and society based on their world view. The grid through which they see the world determines the world they see.

Man makes discoveries about the physical universe and about his physical person: How should he practically apply that knowledge? Man delves into the areas of the mind and spirit: what is real within them and what effect can it have on him? Man establishes institutions and organizations to read and limit his activities and relationships: upon what standards does he base their operation? Does any of that matter? Does man matter? Is he simply part of the cosmic machinery to be explained merely as the apex of the evolutionary process? Is there any meaning to it? Is everything arbitrary? Are there no absolutes? *Is our constantly changing world running out of control? What's your philosophy on "How to handle a world"?*

Debris

"Shock waves" and "Shrapnel" from the time bombs in Part One cause untold wreckage and debris in the psyche of men and women. Most of this debris can be sorted into psychological piles of *fear, anger,* and *guilt.* When the debris is suppressed, it reacts like an embedded splinter, causing aggravated pain! As each pile (fear, anger, guilt) is left unchecked, one builds upon the other creating a devastatingly destructive cycle.

The Deadly Triad!

For example, many parents are extremely uncertain concerning their parental role and responsibilities. As the cultural gap between generations has occurred at shorter and shorter intervals, they find they lack experience in the cultural system their children are growing up in and therefore feel inadequate to give their children guidance.[2] While the parents are trying to "catch-up" with their children, the children are desperately looking for and in need of answers to Why am I? Who am I? Where am I going? and the rights and wrongs of life.

Standing with their feet firmly planted in midair, parents are fearful of being too permissive or too authoritarian. They have been warned from all sides about the damage to the child's psyche that can result from improper rearing, and out of a reservoir of fear they respond in anger to their child's actions. They are not angry at what the child did, but simply that the child did anything at all. The anger is triggered because the child has forced his parents to make a decision in an area of nonconfidence—fear! Their response is, "Why did you do it now!!??" After they've exploded in anger a sense of guilt sets in. This guilt, in turn, produces even more fear, for now they are certain they don't know how to parent! The deadly cycle continues to swirl, disintegrating the relationships, and destroying the people involved.

This deadly triad of debris from the time bombs can be found in varying degrees in every struggle, frustration, and problem people face. It swirls through business, community, and family responsibilities, and through all your relationships from the most casual to the most intimate. Eventually you are forced to face it in the mirror as you are all alone with *you!*

In Part Two we will define the piles of debris of fear, anger, and guilt and illustrate the deadly threesome in several vignettes.

The detonation of these destructive time bombs (Part One) is increasing in intensity with every tick of the clock, and its debris (Part Two) is scattered throughout our world. No one can escape it.

Game-Plan

What we need is a plan (not a box, but a game-plan) for defusing these time bombs personally (Part Three), a game-plan that forces us to search out the answers to the basic questions of life (Why am I? Who am I? Where am I going?) and charts out a course for taking charge of our lives in a responsible way! We need to learn how to get our heads together! We need a mental checkup! *Have you ever had a mental?*

A mental checkup is a plan for discovering the pressure points of life—those areas of stress for which you may later pay with your life! It's a plan that will assist you in discovering *why you are, who you are, and where you are going!* It's a game-plan for life!

The pilot of Midair Airlines announced to the passengers, "Ladies and gentlemen, I have some good news and some bad news. The bad news is our instrumentation has gone out, and we don't know where we're going. The good news is we have picked up a tailwind and are making good time!" It sounds like they're on Humanity Airlines' flight 1980!

Part One

The Detonation of Time Bombs

There was an old woman who lived in a shoe,
She had so many children she didn't know what to do;
She gave them some broth without any bread,
She whipped them all soundly and put them to bed.
There Was an Old Woman

1

The Crowd and the Crud!
Ecological Time Bomb

JOHNNY, A VERY BRIGHT FIVE-YEAR-OLD, told his daddy he'd like to have a baby brother and along with his request offered to do whatever he could to help. His dad, a very bright thirty-five-year-old, paused for a moment and then replied, "I'll tell you what, Johnny. If you pray every night for two months for a baby brother, I guarantee that God will give you one!" (Obviously, dad knew something Johnny didn't.) Johnny responded eagerly to his dad's challenge and went to his bedroom early that night to start praying for a baby brother.

He prayed every night for a whole month, but after that time he began to get skeptical. He checked around the neighborhood, and found out that what he thought was going to happen had never occurred in the history of the neighborhood. You just don't pray for two months and then, whammo! —a new baby brother! So, Johnny quit praying. After another month Johnny's mother went to the hospital. When she came back home, Johnny's parents called him into the bedroom. He cautiously walked into the room, not expecting to find anything, and there was a little bundle lying right next to his mother. His dad pulled back the blanket and there were, not just one baby brother, but two baby brothers—twins! Johnny's dad looked down at him and said, "Now, aren't you glad you prayed?" Johnny hesitated a little and then looked up at his dad and answered, "Yes, but aren't you glad I quit when I did?"

It's a good thing that story is fictitious. Otherwise, another month of Johnny's praying and he would have had four baby brothers! Now, we all know that a child's prayer isn't the determining factor in making babies, but we'd better find out what's causing the increase, or it's going to get crowded! Except for the potential horrors of nuclear war, the population explosion poses the greatest single threat to modern civilization.[1]

The most significant detonator of the *ecological time bomb* is the growth of the world population. Last year it passed four billion, and barring a holocaust brought on by man or nature, right now it is the smallest it will ever be again. How did it reach four billion? For the first 99 percent of man's existence it increased at an amazingly slow rate, but for the last 1 percent of history, its increase has been alarmingly rapid. By 1750, the world's population had only reached about 800 million. Then, as the Industrial Revolution gathered momentum, population growth began to accelerate! By 1900, it had doubled to 1.6 billion; by 1964, it had doubled again to 3.6 billion. Given today's level of complacency in some quarters, and discouragement in others, the likely scenario is for a world stabilized at around eleven billion people.[2]

Doctor Doom

In the late 1960s Paul Ehrlich became a familiar voice on the world scene for his prophetic cries concerning the "population bomb." His message was that the battle to feed all of humanity is over: In the 1970s the world will undergo famines, and in spite of any crash programs now embarked upon, hundreds of millions of people are going to starve to death. At this late date nothing can prevent a substantial increase in the world death rate, although many lives could be saved through dramatic programs to "stretch" the earth's carrying capacity by increasing food production. However, these programs will only provide a stay of execution unless they are accompanied by determined and successful efforts at population control. (Population control is the conscious regulation of numbers of human beings to meet the needs, not just of individual families, but of society as a whole.)

Nothing could be more misleading to children than our present affluent society. The world they inherit will be totally different—a world in which the standards and economics of the 1960s are dead! As the most powerful nation in the world today, and its largest consumer, the United States cannot stand isolated. Today we are involved in the events leading to famine; tomorrow we may be destroyed by its consequences.[3]

Since Ehrlich's warnings, there have been encouraging signs from the developed nations, but the planet's poorest nations have yet to find acceptable and effective ways to check their population increase. India's new government, for example, has abandoned coercive birth control procedures, even though with a present population of 635 million, India is growing by a million new people a month.[4]

After a country has reached an average family size of approximately 2.1 children ("replacement-level fertility"), it may take as long as 70 years before its population stops growing. Even if fertility declined in a typical less-developed country to the 2.1 replacement level by the year 2000, the population would still have increased to 2½ times its current size before stabilizing.[5]

Double Your Money—Your Crowd

The world population is doubling at a present rate of every 37–38 years, and just as interest dollars themselves earn interest, people added to populations produce more people. Because of this principle of interest, populations double in much less time than seems possible. Look at the relationship between the annual percent increase (interest rate) and the doubling time of the population as shown on the next page:

Annual percent increase	Doubling time[6].
1.0	70 years
2.0	35 years
3.0	24 years
4.0	17 years

That's the way your money grows—and the world's population too!

Earth Odyssey—2868 A.D.!

Let's examine what might happen on the absurd assumption that the world's population continues to double every 37 years into the indefinite future.

If growth continued at that rate for about 900 years, there would be some 60,000,000,000,000,000 people on the face of the earth. (Sixty million billion people!) That would be roughly 100 people for every square yard of the earth's surface —land and sea! A British physicist, J.H. Fremlin, postulated that such a multitude might be housed in a continuous 2,000-story building covering the entire planet. The upper 1,000 stories would contain only the apparatus for running the gigantic structure and about half of the space in the bottom 1,000 stories would be occupied with ducts, pipes, wires, elevator shafts, and so on. Because that would leave only three to four yards of floor space for each person, everyone would probably have to be limited in his travel. To be able to move more than a few feet, perhaps people could take the elevators through all 1,000 residential stories, but they could still only travel within a circle of a few hundred yards' radius on any floor. However, everyone would have some ten million people from whom to choose his friends[7]! And that's quite a choice. It's also quite a crowd!

Birth Rate—Death Rate

There are only two basic solutions to the population problem. One is a birth rate, and the other is a "death rate solution," in which ways to raise the death rate—war, famine, pestilence, and so on—find us.[8] Raising the death rate is obviously an undesirable solution, so lowering the birth rate is our only viable solution.

The first major efforts toward bringing about a birth rate solution were made in Holland in 1881 with the opening of the first birth-control clinic, and by the early 1900s they were starting up all over the world. In 1952, after earlier attempts had been thwarted by the disruptions of the two world wars, the International Planned Parenthood Federation (IPPF) was founded in Bombay with the National Family Planning Association of India, the United States, Britain, Hong Kong, Germany, Holland, Sweden, and Singapore as its first members.[9]

Urge to Merge

Birth-control methods range from abstinence to a variety of contraceptives. In most cases the urge to merge eliminates abstinence as an effective birth-control. As for the contraceptives, there are some major factors which also hinder their effectiveness. First, contraceptives must be *used* to be effective, and in the spontaneity of lovemaking many of them remain in the drawer. Second, some contraceptives have become extremely controversial because of their possible negative side effects. These have scared potential users away. Third, research for new, safer, and more convenient contraceptives is prohibitive due to the incredible high cost of governmental approval.

At the present time, requirements by the Federal Food and Drug Administration (FDA) for the approval of a new contraceptive stipulate studies costing between $8 million (government's estimate) and $30 million (private industry's estimate). Even having once expended this amount, a company faces the unpredictable actions of sudden withdrawal of FDA approval or a Senate hearing on the cost of the medication. As a result, many drug firms have discontinued all research in the area of contraceptive technology.[10]

Immigration Explosion

In addition to our native population explosion, we are also experiencing a growth explosion from immigration. Approximately 400,000 *legal* immigrants entered the U.S. in 1974.[11] In that same year the U.S. Immigration and Naturalization Service estimated that 7 to 12 million *illegal* immigrants were also residing in the United States.[12] Illegal immigration is a problem of sizable and growing proportions, with estimates ranging from 400,000 to 1 million or more entering the country every year.[13]

Where Is the Crowd?

The crowd is moving to the cities! In 1975 it was estimated that 25 million people moved from rural areas to towns or cities—most of them to national and provincial capitals. These 25 million additional city dwellers will need extensive new services, education, public transportation, and the other basic necessities of urban living. Whatever can be done to reduce the general growth of population will make this job much easier.[14]

Almost regardless of the existing degree of urbanization, urban centers in Africa, Latin America, and parts of Asia are growing at the rate of 5 to 8 percent yearly. Populations in the developing areas are doubling every 25 to 30 years, but their large cities are only doubling every 10 to 15 years, while their urban slums or shantytowns are doubling every 5 to 7 years.[15]

Urban scholar Lewis Mumford estimates that providing needed services costs three times as much in a large city as in a small town. Yet cities of over a million people are becoming more and more common in developing countries; examples include Shanghai, Peking, Calcutta, Mexico City, Rio de Janeiro, and Sao Paulo.[16]

Before the end of the century, the size of city populations will be radically altered. By the year 2001, perhaps as many as half the world's population will be city-dwellers; and that in a world which will be supporting twice as many people as it was in 1970. Our world is having great and apparently increasing difficulty in feeding, clothing, and housing itself. How shall we accommodate another world on top of this one?[17]

How Old Is the Crowd?

One of the most ominous facts about the current situation is that roughly 40 percent of the undeveloped world's population is made up of people under 15 years old.[18] This means there will be a dramatic rise in the number of young adults from now until about 2985, and that one-third of the expected total population increase will be in the 25 to 34-year-old group. Altogether, there will be an additional 28 million people in their twenties, thirties, and early forties. On the other hand, there will be virtually no change in the number of people between 45 and 64. Of the remaining 16 million persons who are expected to be added to segments of the population in the next 15 years, most will be: preschoolers (8 million), persons over 65 (6 million), and school-age children from 5 to 15 years old (2 million).[19]

Baby: the Superconsumer!

Each baby is, of course, potentially one of the unemployed, but he/she is a consumer nonetheless. It is estimated that each new American will consume or use directly or indirectly, in a 70-year life span: 26 million gallons of water; 21 thousand gallons of gasoline; 10 thousand pounds of meat; 28 thousand pounds of oil and cream; $5,000 to $8,000 in school building materials; $6,300 worth of clothing; and $7,000 worth of furniture. It's not a baby, it's a Superconsumer![20]

Grain—Drain

That we are presently living beyond our means is obvious from the simple fact that we are madly depleting nonreplenishable resources.[21] World grain reserves now amount to only 30 days worth of world consumption. Agricultural production per person in the less developed countries, excluding China, was only 2 percent higher in 1973 than in the early 1960s, even though their total food production was almost 30 percent greater; the increased quantities of food were used primarily to sustain larger numbers at already inadequate nutritional levels. At least ⅔ of the 800 million children in developing countries are expected to experience sickness brought on or aggravated by malnutrition, and it is estimated that between ⅙ and ⅓ of all the deaths that occur in the world each year could have been prevented if the individuals had been properly nourished.[22]

Grain consumed directly provides 52 percent of man's food energy intake. Consumed indirectly in the form of livestock products, it provides a sizeable share of the remainder. In resource terms, grains occupy more than 70 percent of the world's crop area.[23]

H_2O—Going!

The critical grain supplies are dependent on the water supply, up to 120 gallons to grow the grain used in just one loaf of bread. A pound of meat, which requires direct water consumption plus water to grow the animal feed, can require as much as 200 times that amount. Per capita daily water use in the United States has increased more than 75 percent in the last 25 years, and if projected population and per capita consumption trends materialize, world water use is expected to triple by the early twenty-first century.[24]

Going Fishing!

Until the early sixties, when the regenerative capacity of the fishery was pressed beyond its natural limits, haddock were heavily fished as if there were no tomorrow. Then, the catch fell from 249,000 to 23,000 tons, and the price of haddock climbed fourfold within an eight-year period.[25] This strategic source of food is dwindling fast!

Minerals—Going!

Total mineral production during the last 30 years has been greater than it was from the beginning of the Bronze Age until World War II. The United States Bureau of Mines estimates that the world's consumption of aluminum will be twice today's level in 9 years, the use of iron will double in a decade and a half, and that the demand for zinc will double in 17 years.

In 1950, the United States, with 152 million people, depended on foreign sources for more than half of its supplies of only 4 of the 13 basic minerals required by our modern industrial society—bauxite, manganese, nice, and tin. By 1970 potash and zinc had been added to the list.

The projections of the U.S. Department of the Interior indicate that by the end of this century—when the U.S. population is expected to be 265 million—our country will be primarily dependent on imports for its supply of 12 of the 13 minerals, including iron, chromium, copper, lead, sulphur, and tungsten.[26]

The Club of Rome's study, *The Limits of Growth*, estimated that even with a fivefold increase in known reserves, current rates of consumption will exhaust supplies of mercury in 41 years, molybdenum—a key component in steel fabrication—in 65 years, and tungsten in 72 years.[27]

Oil—Going!

World oil extraction has doubled every decade of this century, and it is now depleting every possible reserve.[28] Exportable supplies of oil happened to be concentrated in the hands of a relatively few countries, and when the Organization of Petroleum Exporting Countries (OPEC) realized their strategic position, they quadrupled the price of crude oil. That decision was possibly the most penetrating world-wide move ever made. Everyone was affected!

The Giant Appetite!

At the present time, the United States uses well over half of all the raw materials consumed each year. Think of it! Less than $\frac{1}{15}$ of the world's population requires more than all the rest combined to maintain its inflated position. If the present trend continues, in 20 years we will be much less than $\frac{1}{15}$ of the population, and yet we may be using some 80 percent of all the resources consumed.[29]

Housing—Going!

From one-third to two-thirds of the population of six cities studied for the 1975 World Bank Housing Policy Paper were unable to afford the lowest-cost housing presently being produced: the exact percentages were 35 percent in Hong Kong; 47 percent in Bogota; 55 percent in Mexico City; and close to 65 percent in Madras, Ahmedabad, and Nairobi.[30]

A study from India analyzing income levels, savings capacity, and capital housing costs concluded that 85 percent of Indian households cannot finance ownership of a housing unit. The situation is much the same in other parts of Asia, Africa, Latin America, and southern Europe.

In the United States during the 1950s more than half of all American families were able to buy their own houses. Today, as was also true in the 1920s, only one family in five can afford a nonsubsidized house.[31]

In London, nearly 30,000 squatters, without formal consent, relying on a vague law that dates back to Richard II and the Black Death, are occupying thousands of private dwellings, some forlorn and crumbling, others awaiting new tenants or temporarily vacated by families on holiday (vacation). The squatters contend that the housing shortage, rising rents and inflation have left them no other recourse. Over 200,000 London families are already on waiting lists for housing in public projects.[32]

Soon 80 percent of the low-income urban population of the developing countries, more than half of the world's urban population, will be condemned to live in slums.[33]

Health Care—Going!

For hundreds of millions of people, almost half the world's population, health care is either unavailable or a luxury they cannot afford. Rural Kenya has only one doctor for every 50,000 people. Even if the number of doctors in rural areas tripled in the next 25 years, an expensive and probably unattainable goal, current rates of population growth would still make it impossible to provide the same level of service in the rural areas now offered in the capital city, Nairobi.

A recent survey in Thailand indicated that public health facilities only reach 17 percent of the people. With a population which is expanding at 3 percent a year, or nineteenfold in a century, the portion of the population that never sees a doctor is mushrooming!

In Guatemala, the average citizen visits a hospital or dispensary only once every 15 years. Since there are 6 times as many doctors in the cities as in rural areas, the rapidly growing village population is doomed to life without available medical services.

In Colombia, where the birth rate is 40 per 1000 and the infant mortality rate is high, an effort was made to improve health care by constructing a center for the care of premature babies in the capital of Bogota. In this facility, one of the first anywhere, the number of infant deaths has been reduced to a European level. Unfortunately, because of the large number of babies born every year, the children cannot continue to receive the same excellent care after they leave the hospital. Consequently, almost three-fourths of the infants who receive special treatment there die within 3 months after they return home.[34]

Recreation Areas—Going!

Ski slopes, golf courses, beaches, city parks, wildlife preserves, and campgrounds are all utilized by increasing numbers of people each year. Access to what some view as a public resource has become an increasingly sensitive issue as the world's pressures push its expanding population out to enjoy the therapy of nature. Yet all too often what people find is the same congestion they left behind—bumper-to-bumper traffic, noise, air pollution, and crowded, overflowing recreation areas. The impossibility of leaving behind the problems of the city plagues both the affluent and underdeveloped countries alike.[35]

Can't See the Forest for the Trees Are Going!

The number of vanishing forests (deforestation) is on the increase throughout the world! The two principle causes of deforestation are directly linked to population growth:

land clearing for agriculture and wood gathering for fuel. Tree harvesting for lumber is a third, but globally less significant, source of deforestation.

Nine-tenths of the people in most of the poorest countries today depend on firewood as their chief source of fuel, and all too often the growth in human population is outstripping the growth of new trees. This isn't surprising, considering the average villager needs nearly a ton of firewood a year.[36]

Crowd→Crud!

The world's growing crowd is consuming everything imaginable and at an astonishing rate. It's becoming increasingly impossible to replenish the supplies to keep up with the demand. And we not only have a crowd to cope with, we must also have the crud produced by the crowd.

Cruddy Water→Diseases!

Once beautiful Lake Erie became a virtual septic tank—a stinking pool of pollution.[36] The Mediterranean Sea now serves as the sewer system for over 400 million people, and although its ecological balance had never been seriously jeopardized until the mid-twentieth century, overpopulation, the tourist boom, industrial development, and maritime irresponsibility now threaten to turn it into another Dead Sea. Increasingly larger bodies of water are being saturated with waste. In the words of Thor Hyerdahl, "We began to realize that the ocean has something in common with all other bodies of water: it's vulnerable."[38]

Human pollution can be either biological or chemical—both are devastating. The burden of chemical pollution has been felt in the Baltic Sea and Lake Superior. In an effort to improve the water quality of the Ruhr River, in the Federal Republic of Germany, the neighboring river of Emscher has been officially sanctioned as a dumping ground for untreated industrial waste. In Minamata Bay, Japan, the release of industrial waste mercury into fishing waters has led to several thousand cases of a mind-numbing, limb-twisting sickness, now called Minamata disease.[39]

In areas of high population concentration, growing demands on water resources has helped set the stage for outbreaks of cholera, typhoid, and hepatitis. Two-thirds of the population in the poor countries lack access to safe water, and the construction of pure water services continues to lag behind the growth in demand.[40]

Schistosomiasis is a debilitating, water-based parasitic illness present in 71 countries, and it affects a population equal to that of the United States. Described as "the greatest plague in the world" by the U.S. Public Health Service, it is spread by microscopic parasites carried by snails that thrive in irrigation water polluted by human waste. In many nations it has already reached epidemic proportions. For example, in Egypt, a country of fifteen million people, two out of every five people are infected with the parasite.[40] We need more clean water!

How about desalting the ocean?

If the rosiest predictions of the commercial interests working on desalting come true, we will have a worldwide desalting capacity of 20 billion gallons a day in 1984. That's encouraging, and pretty impressive, until you learn that the U.S. alone will need 600 billion gallons of water a day in 1984—two-thirds more than the 360 billion gallons used today.[42]

Cruddy Air→A New Ice Age?

At the moment it is impossible to predict what the overall climatic results will be due to our using the atmosphere as a garbage dump. The multi-actions of the crowd generate quite a quantity of dust alone in the atmosphere. Some scientists fear that increased amounts of atmospheric dust may act as insulation reflecting the sun's rays away from the earth and lowering temperatures. Studies of the glaciers indicate that high concentrations of dust in the air were associated with the onset of the last ice age.

While rising atmospheric dust levels may be cooling the earth, another pollutant, carbon dioxide, appears to be exerting a warming influence. Called "green-house effect," it slows down the release of the earth's heat into space. According to the best estimates, carbon dioxide levels have increased 10–15 percent since the beginning of this century.[43]

We do know that in either direction even very small changes in the average temperature of the earth could be very serious. With a few degrees of cooling, a new ice age might begin, having rapid and drastic effects on the agricultural productivity of the temperate regions. With a few degrees of heating the polar ice caps would melt, which could raise the earth's ocean levels 250 feet.[44]

Cruddy Air→Breath of Death

Welcome to Los Angeles, where you can wake up every morning to the sound of birds—coughing! Dust, sulphur dioxide, and other by-products resulting from the burning of fossil fuels have been directly linked to illness and death. A recent study conducted in Nashville, Tennessee, showed that the incidence of heart disease in polluted areas was nearly double the normal rate. A similar study of nonsmokers in California indicated that men who live in cities die of lung cancer over three times as often as their counterparts in relatively unpolluted areas.[45] Workplace pollutants—arsenic, asbestos, polyvinyl chloride, and others—have been found to be carcinogenic agents![46]

With this in mind maybe the best new market for sales is a handsome-looking gas mask. They may be as common as sunglasses someday!

Cruddy Vibrations→Huh???

Although environmentalists, ethologists, biologists, and even politicians have continued to predict the potential damages of high density living—and even go so far as to assert that crowding causes tension, anxiety, aggressiveness, divorce, family troubles, neurosis, and crime—little research has been focused directly on the effects of crowding on humans. However, extensive research has been done on how crowding affects animals, and the results strongly suggest that humans are adversely affected by high population density.[47]

In the U.S., the crime rate in big cities is more that five times higher than in small cities, eight times higher than in the suburbs, and eleven times higher than in rural areas.[48]

Crowding and its side effects, competition and aggression, can induce stressful situations. This stress seems to be a major factor governing susceptibility to high blood pressure and heart disease, skin disorders and stroke, and behavioral problems such as child abuse, alcoholism, and homicide.

Apart from the stress caused by crowding, Philip Simbardo, a Stanford University psychologist, believes that the uncivil behavior of New Yorkers stems from feelings of anonymity or "deindividuation," the feeling that, "If no one knows who I am, what difference does it make what I do?" Stress transforms neighbors into enemies; it generates fear, insecurity in friendships, and rude behavior.[49]

The *ecological time bomb* keeps on ticking! What, then, is being done overall to nurse our sick environment back to health? How well are we treating these symptoms of the earth's disease of overpopulation? Are we guarding the natural cycles on which our lives depend? Are we protecting ourselves from subtle and chronic poisoning? The answer so far is obvious—the attempts are too few and too weak. The patient continues to get sicker![50]

In many ways what is being done to defuse this time bomb is like putting a band-aid on a hemorrhage!

Ring around the rosy,
A pocket full of posies.
Ashes, Ashes,
We all fall down!
Ring Around the Rosy

2

You Are What You Eat: The Chemical Time Bomb

POOR JOHNSON HAD SPENT his life making wrong decisions. If he bet on a horse, it would lose; if he chose one elevator rather than another, it was the one he chose that stalled between floors; the line he picked before the bank teller's cage never moved; the lane he chose in traffic crawled; the day he picked for a picnic there was a cloudburst; and so it went, day after day, year after year.

Then, once, it became necessary for Johnson to travel to some city a thousand miles away and do it quickly. A plane was the only possible conveyance that would get him there in time, and it turned out that only one company supplied only one flight that would do. His heart bounded. There was no choice to make; and if he made no choice, surely he could come to no grief.

He took the plane.

Imagine his horror when, midway in the flight, the plane's engines caught fire and it became obvious the plane would crash in moments.

Johnson broke into fervent prayer to his favorite saint, Saint Francis. He pleaded, "I have never in my life made the right choice. Why this should be, I don't know, but I have borne my cross and have not complained. On this occasion, however, I did not make a choice; this was the only plane I could take and I had to take it. Why, then, am I being punished?"

He had no sooner finished than a giant hand swooped down out of the clouds and somehow snatched him from the plane. There he was, miraculously suspended two miles above the earth's surface, while the plane spiraled downward far below.

A heavenly voice came down from the clouds. "My son, I can save you, if you have in truth called upon me."

"Yes, I called on you," cried Johnson. "I called on you, Saint Francis."

"Ah," said the heavenly voice, "Saint Francis Xavier or Saint Francis of Assisi. Which?"

In each of the time bombs there is a lot of ambivalence—good news and bad news—and the chemical time bomb is no exception! *Good news:* Honey is good for you! *Bad news:* 40 percent of all honey on the market today may be fatal to children under a year old. *Good news:* sodium nitrite, used in hot dogs, bacon, lunch meat, and so on, prevents botulism! *Bad news:* sodium nitrite can cause cancer! *Good news:* Saccharin, an artificial sweetener, can be used as a substitute for harmful sugar. *Bad news:* Saccharin can also cause cancer! You're doomed if you do and doomed if you don't! You can't seem to win!

Chemicals: Food Contamination

Whether you live to eat or eat to live, you are faced with the problem of food contamination. There is an enormous number of different types of chemicals that can theoretically contaminate food. It has been estimated that some 1 to 2 million chemical compounds currently originate from industrial processes, and the more persistent of these could well find their way into the ecosystem and eventually into our food. Essentially, there are three categories of environmental food contaminants: (1) those introduced by agricultural technology, (2) those introduced by industrial pollution, and (3) those which have naturally occurred. A fourth category, contaminants formed during food processing, is not strictly applicable, although the precursors could be environmental in origin.[1]

Two questions must be answered to define a poisonous contaminant in foods: How much is present, and how toxic is that amount? Food doesn't reach the consumer until it has been through a long chain of preparation and processing operations, during which it can be contaminated by chemicals. These chemicals are not present intentionally, as are food additives, but are the unavoidable results of technological operations, as well as from environmental pollution, natural sources, or sometimes just sheer carelessness.[3]

Chemicals: Food Additives

A food additive is a substance added to food either directly and intentionally for a functional purpose, or indirectly during some phase of production, processing, storage or packaging without intending that it remain in or serve a purpose in, the final product. It does not include either the basic foodstuff or chance contaminants.

In other words, intentional additives are substances purposely added to perform specific functions. Incidental additives are substances which are present in trace quantities as a result of some phase of production, processing, storage or packaging.[4]

Although manufactured additives are frequently and sometimes critically called "chemicals," they are no more so than those made by nature. All additives, whether they come from natural or man-made sources, are "chemicals." In fact, technically speaking, everything in the world is chemical—all the substances in food, clothing, shelter, and even the earth and its inhabitants are chemical.[5]

As we are bombarded with incessant warnings of the chemical vs. the natural, it's easy to be overcome with the feeling that everything is filled with "harmful chemicals" and depleted of anything "healthy" and/or "natural." However, the facts just aren't there to prove that. Our per capita consumption of food in 1970 was 1500 pounds, of which only 5 pounds were additives of all kinds. Even the most controversial chemicals—synthetic food colors that are used in dairy products, beverages, baked goods, spices, jellies, candy, cereals, meat-product casings, and maraschino cherries—are consumed in very small quantities. According to the National Academy of Sciences/National Research Council, the total consumption of these is only about 0.012 pounds (5.5 grams) per person every year.[6]

Please Don't Eat the Wrappers!

If it weren't for food additives, baked goods would go stale and mold overnight, salad dressings would separate and turn rancid, table salt would turn hard and lumpy, canned fruits and vegetables would become discolored and mushy, vitamin potencies would deteriorate, beverages and frozen desserts would lack flavor, and wrappings would stick to their contents.[7]

The first nutrient supplement to be added to food was iodine. The value of this additive was proved when it was discovered that the use of iodized salt can prevent simple goiter. A few years later in the 1930s milk was first fortified with vitamin D. This came after scientists had discovered that it helps prevent rickets, the childhood disease in which bones are not formed properly.[8]

Mold, bacteria, and yeast all cause food spoilage, as most homemakers know. Not only are these microorganisms capable of spoiling the palatability of foods, but some of them may also create serious illness in man. Salmonella and botulism are examples of microorganisms that are known to be toxic. Food additives are necessary to prevent these and other diseases.[9]

When Eating Is Against the Law

The first major legislation regulating food in this country was the Federal Food and Drug Act passed in 1906. The purpose of pure food legislation was summed up by the late George P. Larrick, former Commissioner of Food and Drugs,

Department of Health, Education, and Welfare: "Federal food laws for more than half a century have been dedicated to safety, wholesomeness, and the type of labeling that will permit citizens to make intelligent selections in their purchases. Telling people what to eat is attempted by education rather than regulation. Their choices affect the whole food industry, for in the long run the practices of manufacturers reflect consumers' wishes."[10]

After years of legislation hearings and countless revisions, the Federal Food, Drug, and Cosmetic Act of 1938 was adopted. The fair-packaging and labeling act, enacted in 1966 as an amendment to the 1938 Act, was designed to provide consumers with adequate information about product ingredients, including net weight and quantity to enable them to make value comparisons.[11]

New and revised laws and amendments are amassing with regard to food production, preparation, packaging, and distribution. There are now more than 1250 federal advisory boards, committees, commissions, and councils regulating the food business. In 1970 the Environmental Protection Agency was established to supervise these agencies and ensure the enforcement of their regulations.

Since its inception the EPA and other governmental regulatory agencies have been under fire for their "endless" restrictions, many of which appear to defy common sense. A popular example is the saccharin ban issued in 1977 by the Food and Drug Administration. Because of the high usage of saccharin as a sugar substitute, the announcement that it was carcinogenic then produced quite a scare. As the research and evidence to justify such a ban (and scare) were examined more closely, the attacks began to mount.

Poor Future—Being a Rat

The FDA's announced ban on saccharin was based on a Canadian study which involved feeding 100 rats a diet of 5 percent pure saccharin for their entire lives, from conception until death. The result was that 14 of those rats developed cancerous bladder tumors, compared with only 2 such tumors in a group of 100 animals given no saccharin.[12] There's no doubt about it, rats are definitely taking a chance by eating saccharin!

But what about people? Does it make sense to ban a popular food additive on the basis of what happens when a hundred rats and their offspring eat the additive in huge doses?[13] To consume an equivalent amount of saccharin, the FDA said, a person would have to drink 800 12-ounce diet sodas a day for a lifetime![14]

Hardly any of the food you eat can withstand the kind of testing new products are being subjected to today to prove their so-called innocence. Eggs, for instance, when fed in fairly large quantities to rats, cause cancer. And how about the old saying, "An apple a day keeps the doctor away"? Apples contain four naturally occurring chemicals that are on the National Institute of Science and Health's list of suspected carcinogens. No more apples; No more eggs! No more food! It's the new "Terminal Diet"![15]

When a Bug Becomes a Pest

The first and most basic question that needs to be asked in connection with any insect is: Is it a pest? There are approximately 800,000 species of insects known to man and only a few of them have been defined as pests. Unfortunately, the public has been so conditioned to think of all small creatures as pests that their initial response to insects has often been fear and hatred, and consequently a move to kill as many of them as possible.[16]

The most significant problem of bugs becoming pests is in the agricultural arena. Because pests do kill crops, farmers are forced to discover ways of killing them. Hence, the pesticide!

Chemical pesticides and fertilizers—along with major advances in farm mechanization and plant genetics—have enabled the American farmer to achieve a miraculous increase in productivity during the twentieth century. The same amount of acres harvested to feed about 80 million Americans in 1910 produced enough food to feed some 200 million

Americans in 1970.[17] Along with increased land usage has also come a decrease in food costs. It's been estimated that by using chemical pesticides to maximize agricultural production, farmers save Americans over $20 billion a year on their grocery bills.[18]

Pests: Bugs, Weeds, Fungi, Rodents, Worms, Snails

The general term pesticide is applied to a variety of pest control measures, including *insecticides* for killing "bugs," *herbicides* for weeds, *fungicides* for fungi, *rodenticides* for rodents, *nematocides* for wormlike organisms, and *molluscides* for snails.[19]

Atom Bomb and DDT!

The atom bomb and DDT were first used in World War II, and the discovery of both nuclear fission and the pesticide received Nobel prizes in the 1940s. During the past 25 years, pesticides and nuclear energy have moved from the military to the civilian world, and in the process these two technologies have become the best known and perhaps most widespread sources of global pollution. The big cry of "Ban the bomb" has been joined by "Ban the bug bomb" in languages all around the world.[20]

DDT is one of the various pesticides which has the unfortunate characteristic of persisting in the environment. These persistent, or so-called "hard" pesticides, do not easily break down into less harmful components. Instead they retain their toxicity long after application and present an ever increasing problem.[21]

Pesticide Scare!

DDT is now present in rain and surface water in concentrations of only parts per trillion, but most people carry it in their fatty tissues at a level of a million times higher, between five and twenty parts per million. There are few foods, if any, in the human diet which are free from DDT, and recent studies show that even a mother's milk passes some DDT to the infant.[22]

Pesticides are hazardous for a variety of reasons. Many are highly suspect as being possible causes of cancer. Some are regarded as potential inducers of birth defects in man. There are also indications that certain pesticides could have the power to alter heredity material, producing genetic change and affecting future generations![23]

Birds and mammals share similar sex hormones and have much the same apparatus for regulating their metabolism. Evidence that environmental levels of DDT are affecting bird reproduction therefore raises the question of whether man and other high animals are also suffering from its subtle effects.[24]

Pesticide Scare Scare!

But wait a minute! There's another side to the pesticide scare which is even scarier than the first to many people—the pesticide scare scare! It's the fear that the pesticide scare has been blown out of proportion without the evidence to back it up!

In a recent article entitled "Of Mites and Men," William Tucker, a contributing editor to Harper's, revealed some interesting evidence with reference to the DDT controversy. He pointed out that DDT has been known for many years not to cause any noticeable increase in cancer. Among the thousands and thousands of factory hands, pesticide sprayers, farm workers, and people in malaria-prone underdeveloped countries who have been heavily exposed over the course of thirty-five years, there has *never* been suffered accidental exposure great enough to put them in the hospital. In the 1950s, volunteers even ate large quantities of DDT in a series of tests and never suffered any adverse effects.

Most of these facts were known during the late 1960s when environmentalists determined to show that DDT was a public health menace. To solve their problem, they invented a kind of intellectual game which stated that, although there was no evidence to show that DDT did cause cancer, it was *philosophically impossible* for anyone to show that it couldn't cause cancer.[25]

The environmentalists are supporting a zero-risk philosophy while the scientists are advocating a risk-benefit philosophy says that we must take certain risks to benefit from new discoveries, and it does have the past examples of increased agricultural production, increased life expectancy, healthful food preparation and packaging, and prevention of disease, to back it up. All the zero-risk philosophy has successfully done so far is to bring new research to a screeching halt!

Whether you take the side of the scientists or the environmentalists, these sobering realities remain. (1) There are more insect pest species today than ever before. (2) Over 200 of these species have developed a resistance to chemicals. (3) Pesticides are polluting the biosphere. (4) The cost of pest control continues to climb.[26]

The EPA recently provided a U.S. Court of Appeals judge with some interesting data relating to the Federal Insecticide, Fungicide, and Rodenticide Act: (1) in 1975 the EPA received 5,441 applications for registration of new products; 2,850 (52 percent) were granted. (2) In 1977, the number of applications plunged to 1,763, and only 103 (6 percent) registrations were issued. What these numbers *don't* show is that all 103 of those 1977 registrations were only refinements approved by the EPA. The actual number of new registrations since mid-1976 is *zero!*[27]

Chemicals: Air Pollution

Approximately 264 million tons of pollutants are discharged into the air by the United States in a year. This aerial garbage consists of about 23 million tons of nitrogen oxides, 35 million tons of hydrocarbons, 34 million tons of sulfur oxides, 26 million tons of particulates, and 147 million tons of carbon monoxide.

Transportation sources, primarily automobiles, contribute about 144 million tons—including almost 111 million tons of carbon monoxide, 20 million tons of hydrocarbons, and 12 million tons of nitrogen oxides.

Industrial processes and fuel burning at power plants and other stationary sources produce about 81 million tons of pollutants. The remainder comes from burning solid wastes, agriculture refuse, coal scraps, and miscellaneous sources.[28]

Air Pollution Kills People

An air pollution episode occurs when adverse weather conditions, usually low winds and a temperature inversion, cause abnormally high concentrations of pollutants to build up in the air. Donora, Pennsylvania, suffered the first recorded air pollution episode in the United States in 1948. Stagnant air, fog, and factory fumes combined to blanket the small industrial town in a thick black smog. Before the air was cleared by wind and rain four days later, 20 people were dead. More than 5,900 of the town's 14,000 people became ill with coughs, sore throats, difficult breathing, irritated eyes, nausea, and vomiting.

Other cities have also suffered such episodes. London has had several: One in 1873 took 650 lives; the worst, in 1952, caused 4000 deaths and sickened many thousands more. New York City has also had several episodes; one in 1963 caused between 200 and 400 deaths.[29]

Air Pollution Kills Money

The EPA estimates that air pollution takes a $6.1 billion a year toll on human health in the form of illness, lost time, medical bills, and premature death. Damage to crops and vegetation is estimated at $100 million a year; damage to materials at $4.7 billion; and damage to residential property, $5.2 billion yearly. The total estimated cost of air pollution is therefore $16.1 billion a year, and most agree that is a conservative estimate.

Other studies have put the cost of air pollution even higher, adding $200 a year per person in heavily polluted areas, and $850 a year per family in New York City for extra cleaning, household maintenance, and personal care.[30]

Comparing the cost of damages from air pollution with the

cost of controlling it—about 1.65 billion a year—indicates that air pollution control is a bargain. In fact, based upon available estimates, air pollution control would produce a net gain of $5.45 billion a year for the American people.[31]

Chemicals: Water Pollution

After various degrees of treatment or no treatment at all municipal sewer systems discharge into our waterways some 40 billion gallons of effluent a day. Industry discharges at least 125 billion gallons of effluent a day, the majority of it untreated, and agricultural operations another 50 billion gallons, which is almost entirely untreated.[32]

Federal officials have tallied how many of the 260,000 stream miles in our major drainage basins are markedly polluted. In the early 1970s it amounted to almost one mile out of every three.[33]

All of this dirty water causes disease for people as well as rats! In the decade of the 1960s there were 130 officially recorded outbreaks of disease in this country caused by drinking water—more than one a month—involving as many as 16,000 individual episodes.[34]

Ambivalence!

Ambivalence? Yes, the pros and cons from the scientists and environmentalists will produce ambivalent feelings! But these ambivalent feelings are certainly better than the bureaucratic absurdity created by the U.S. Government. Their separation of environmental pollution problems into isolated categories does provide a functional convenience, but it's also a biological absurdity.

In the federal government, air pollution control is the province of the National Air Pollution Control Administration under the Department of Health, Education, and Welfare. Water Pollution control is the province of the Federal Water Pollution Control Administration under the Department of the Interior. The Atomic Energy Commission (not under any Department) is in charge of encouraging the development of nuclear energy and of protecting the environment and its inhabitants from the effects of radioactive by-products when they have been emitted into the air. Pesticides, which can also become both air and water pollutants, are regulated by the Department of Agriculture. The protection of forests is divided between the National Park Service under the Department of the Interior and the Forest Service under the Department of Agriculture.[35]

Much of the authority for the detailed regulation of air and water pollution is in the hands of numerous state, county, and municipal agencies with each department accumulating regulations and restrictions in their particular area. Meanwhile the chemical time bomb continues to tick away through contamination and corruption, and the masses continue to make messes!

Mary, Mary quite contrary,
How does your garden grow?
With silver bells, and cockle shells,
And pretty maids all in a row.
Mary, Mary Quite Contrary

3

Beauty and the Beast: The Biological Time Bomb

WHENEVER I THINK OF BIOLOGY I picture myself back in a college lab trying to dissect various assorted creatures. I'm also reminded of the story about the student who was preparing for a biology exam. The class had been studying, dissecting, and examining all kinds of animals during the semester: frogs, worms, birds, rats, cats, and so on. Being a conscientious student, Jerry had read and reread his notes, and when the day of reckoning arrived he felt thoroughly prepared!

As the students quieted down in preparation for the exam the professor pulled a surprise on them. Instead of handing out the usual lab exam, he arranged five cages on the front table with a cloth partially draped over each cage. The only thing the class could see were the legs of five different birds. The exam was to identify each of the birds by viewing their legs! Everyone sat there in shock! Jerry was furious. The exam had little or nothing to do with either the material or experiments they had covered. It seemed totally absurd!

Jerry did attempt to identify the birds, but his frustration level soon reached a saturation point! He got up, marched over to the professor's desk, slammed his test paper down, and blurted out, "This is the most ridiculous examination I have ever taken. It has absolutely *nothing* to do with what we have been studying in this class!"

Having vented his frustration, Jerry stormed toward the door. The professor yelled after him, "Wait a minute, young man! What's your name?" Jerry turned around, leaned against the doorway, raised both his pants legs and said, "It's your turn, prof, *you* guess!"

It would be a lot easier if the biological time bomb only consisted of frustrating exams about birds. Unfortunately, it's a frustrating exam about people! The questions seem to be impossible, and yet the answers to them are critical: Abortion? Euthanasia? Test-tube babies? Postponing death? Sexual necessity? Creation of life? Mind control? A brain without a body? *Where are we going? What will we become?* In the early months of 1971 the first shock waves of the biological bomb, which had exploded in scientific circles, began to be felt by the public. Before that time only scientists and intellectuals who were up on the latest developments in molecular physics, biochemistry, and genetics knew what was happening or had any indication of the implications for the future. As popular journals in Europe and the United States started carrying news story after news story about the discoveries in the life sciences, a revolution began which is raising questions for human society previously considered only by science fiction writers and professional futurologists.[1]

Biology has just reached the critical point of sudden acceleration—which was reached by physics a generation ago—and the biological time bomb is about to explode in our faces! Life, a living, self-duplicating organism, is created in the laboratory from inert chemicals! A child is born a hundred years after his father's death! Scores of human beings are brought into the world by a process in which sex plays no part! Death is indefinitely postponed by deep-freeze! Genetic control of intelligence, mood, and memory! *How far will man go in tampering with the functions of nature?*[2]

Who's in Control?

In this generation we are rapidly moving our decision making from the individual to his society. The bonds linking the individual to society, which have become progressively more predominant, are becoming stronger than those which sustain his personal strategy. Man's inner nature is becoming the consequence of a social decision, and society is swallowing up the control of the individual.[3]

Who's in control? This is a major question concerning each of the time bombs, but it is especially relevant to the biological. The biological time bomb can be viewed most clearly through its progressive degree of control:

    I. Not to have life—Not to have death
    II. To have life
    III. Not to have defective life
    IV. To have life as desired

I. Not to Have Life—Not to Have Death

Not to have life can be approached in three different ways: contraception, abortion, and euthanasia. *Contraception is not to have life by preventing its creation.* In spite of the moral and religious attacks made upon them, contraceptives have experienced widespread acceptance. In the late 1960s a survey showed that 21 percent of American Roman Catholic women under the age of 45 had used birth-control pills, and that percentage is much greater now, not only for the pill but for other contraceptives as well. This means that as soon as a technique is developed which is convenient and not offensive to personal taboos, it will be adopted, regardless of theological or moralistic considerations.[4]

Abortion is not to have life by stopping it after conception but before birth. Even though abortion has now been legalized, the debate between those for and against it continues. The arguments revolve around the moral question as to when and whether one can justify destroying the fetus. The underlying issue is whether or not the fetus is a human being with the right to be protected.[5] The controversy over abortion laws rests on grounds of a private, personal religious conviction and therefore should not be established by government in violation of the Constitution's first amendment.[6]

Euthanasia is not to have life by terminating it after creation and birth. If an embryo is in the way, abortion is the answer! If an old person is in the way, euthanasia is the answer! Abortion is here, and euthanasia is following close behind it. Dr. Francis Crick, the scientist who unravelled the DNA code along with Dr. James D. Watson, is recognized as one of the most outstanding men in the area of biology. Dr. Crick strongly implies that we must rethink what kind of people we want in society, and then learn to tinker with the system until we can decide who should be born and who should die. To him it's a moral necessity![7]

Not to have death is primarily concerned with "arrested death" and "deep-freeze." Arrested death keeps a person from dying by maintaining the vital signs with the use of machines. The body continues to function, even though there is a loss of consciousness. In 1966 an 11-year-old girl died in a hospital in Liverpool. Six years earlier, when she was only 5, she had been run over by a car. At enormous cost a team of skilled physicians had kept her in a state of arrested death. With the increase of research knowledge people can be kept in this "living" prison for an indefinite period of time, perhaps someday for ever.[8]

Deep-freeze is another way not to have death. The proposal that human beings be preserved alive by freezing offers people suffering from an incurable disease the possibility of waiting around until a cure is discovered. If a person who died of pneumonia in 1920 had been preserved until today, he could almost certainly have been saved.

If the process proved to be free from risk, others might wish to store themselves for a while, to see the world of the future, or how their children turned out, or simply because they had a passionate desire to know the answer to some unsolved problem. If they didn't like the world they found when they "unfroze," they could presumably return to the freezer for another period of storage. But the social consequences of deep-freeze, both positive and negative, are so complicated and far-reaching that it is well worth evaluating its practicability very carefully.[9]

A facet of the deep-freeze concept that may be more feasible is induced hibernation—a slowing of the body processes rather than a complete cessation. After all, we know this is possible: nature does it naturally.[10]

"Not to have life" must wrestle with the question, "What is life?" "Not to have death" has to wrestle with the question, "What is death?" We must all wrestle with the question, "Who will decide?"

II. To Have Life

The second progressive degree of control in the biological time bomb is *to have life,* and this is where true genetic engineering begins! The popular term, genetic engineering, is often used for anything having to do with the manipulation of the gametes of fetus, from conception by means other than sexual union, to the treatment of disease in the embryo in the uterus to the ultimate manufacture of a human being to exact specifications. Actually genetic engineering has nothing to do with the creation of life; it is concerned only with the method of transmitting life. The simplest procedure in genetic engineering is artificial insemination, next artificial fertilization, and then artificial implantation. Extracorporeal gestation follows and ultimately, cloning, what is popularly meant by genetic engineering, the production—or biological manufacture—of a human being to desired specifications.[11]

Genetic engineering includes the whole spectrum of knowledge associated with cloning (culturing from a cell or group of cells), in vitro fertilization (fertilization occurring in the lab outside of the organism), molecular genetics, genetic counseling, medical genetics, and eugenics (improvement of the quality of a race), environmental factors affecting heredity.[12]

Artificially Manufactured!

Any attempt at producing a live baby by means of laboratory fertilization and culture must be called "experimental" in the sense of being new and untested, full of uncertainties and unknown hazards. Yet the use of untested, potentially hazardous procedures is often justified if the purpose is therapeutic (i.e. "nonexperimental"), and if the potential therapeutic benefits are thought to outweigh the possible risks. But just exactly where is the fine line separating the therapeutic from the "experimental"?[13]

Owing to the work of microbiologists and embryologists, parents who are separated by space or even by death can conceive babies, women can nourish and gestate other women's children, one man can "father" thousands of children, and babies can be shaped—not only by the seed of man—but also by genetic intervention. Also owing to their work, virgin births or parthenogenesis (for that's what cloning is) are expected to be possible in the near future, along with biochemists' and pharmacologists' projection of artificial wombs and placentas. All of which means we are either going to have to change or at least alter our old ideas about who or what is a father or a mother or a family.[15]

III. Not to Have Defective Life

The third progressive degree of control in the biological time bomb is *not to have defective life*. Defective life caused by birth defects or diseases is extensive. There are at least 1500 distinguishable human diseases already known to be genetically determined, and new ones are being found each year. While the molecular basis for most of these diseases is not yet understood, a recent review identified 92 human disorders for which a genetically determined specific enzyme deficiency has been found responsible.[16]

About 5 percent of all babies born in the United States have some kind of congenital defect. This means that about 45 to 50 of every 1000 newborns will have a defect due either to an error in the genetic message or to some imperfection produced by the prenatal environment. Another estimate of the extent of genetically induced birth defects indicates that more than 2 percent of the population suffers from defects or diseases which are inherited.[17]

In the case of birth defects, this represents over 36 million future life years lost. When this is compared with the future life years lost due to heart disease, cancer, and strokes, birth defects will claim approximately 4.5 times as many life years as heart disease, 8 times as many as cancer, and about 10 times as many as strokes.[18]

To give assistance in understanding and treating birth defects and diseases, genetic counseling and genetic surgery have been created.

The purpose of genetic counseling is "to disseminate understanding and knowledge concerning genetic problems as they arise." This field has been strengthened with prenatal genetic diagnosis and the amount of information it has made available concerning the developing fetus. Amniocentesis, a technique for withdrawing fluid from the amniotic cavity, is the principal means for discerning possible genetic disorders of the developing embryo. The data which is gathered can be helpful in confirming or negating the presence of genetic disease and for monitoring the life functions of a fetus developing at risk as a result of maternal deficiencies (as in RH blood factor).[19]

Genetic surgery is progressing rapidly, and each week the media reports on its latest developments. When the viral DNA was synthesized, the techniques became available to begin working on the synthesis of other more complex forms of DNA. As the coding sequence of DNA in higher organisms is deciphered, the more complex DNA can then be synthesized to duplicate or modify its natural forms. The opportunity would then be present with possible application even to man, to substitute the synthesized DNA for the natural DNA in the egg, sperm, or body cell and thus regulate the development of life.[20]

For the first time doctors can take pictures of a single gene, among the millions in a human cell, and see if an unborn baby is missing any parts in its genetic blueprint. Scientists estimate there are 3 to 4 million genes in each human cell, and they are able to isolate and identify the one gene that controls hemoglobin. With this information doctors can act before birth while the child is still developing in the womb.[21]

IV. To Have Life As Desired

Not to have life—Not to have death, to have life, not to have defective life, and finally *to have life as desired.* At this final point in the progressive degrees of control "true eugenics" begins.

Eugenics is the study and control of various possible influences as a means of improving the heredity characteristics of a race. Negative eugenics is concerned with the prevention of mating between individuals possessing inferior or undesirable traits. Positive eugenics is concerned with promotion of optional mating between individuals possessing superior or desirable traits.[22]

One recent controversial issue has been the genetic irregularity known as the XYY defect in which the male has an extra Y chromosone. Various studies have suggested that there might be a relationship between criminal behavior and this genetic abnormality.[23] "Sorry, Judge, I couldn't help it. It's in my genes!"

Eugenics is the attempt to create intelligent, productive, healthy, beautiful, and kind people. It sounds like a similar attempt made 40 years ago at creating a "super-race"! *How far will we go with it?*

Gene Pollution

It is entirely possible, considering the present increasing pollution of the human gene pool through uncontrolled sexual reproduction, that we might have to replicate healthy people both to compensate for the spread of genetic diseases and to elevate the plus factors available in ordinary reproduction. Overpopulation could force us to put a stop to general fecundity (abundant production power), and then, to avoid discrimination, to resort to laboratory fertilization from unidentified cell sources.[24]

Test Tube Baby—It's a Girl

"In vitro" fertilization, the technical name for the conception of a baby in a laboratory rather than in the female reproductive tract, has now succeeded. The first test tube baby was born July 25, 1978, in Oldham, England. It was a girl!

Simply stated, the procedure involves removing a woman's egg at the critical time of month, when it is susceptible to fertilization, placing it in a laboratory dish, and then adding the husband's sperm. If the egg becomes fertilized, the resulting embryo is nurtured in the dish for about four and one-third days, until it has reached what is called the blastocyst stage of development, and then reimplanted in the mother's uterus. If this procedure is succesful, the embryo will attach itself to the uterine wall and develop in the normal fashion. Each of these steps requires precise timing and careful attention; for example, to the temperature and the chemical makeup of the fluids in the dish.[25]

Dr. Jean Rostand, the French biologist, commented on the advent of test-tube babies, "it will be little more than a game to change the subject's sex, the color of its eyes, the general proportions of body and limbs, and perhaps the facial features." "The man-farming biologist," he added, might well be tempted to tamper with the intellectual makeup of the subject as well, predetermining, *a la* Huxley, the behavior and attitudes of an individual for a lifetime.[26]

Pretty Maidens All in a Row—Cloning?

Cloning has been associated in the mind of the layman, and in scientific articles as well, with the possibility of "fabricating man" or producing large numbers of identical individuals by tissue culture techniques.

If this technique is examined in the same light as many of the other developments in genetics and embryology, cloning is then visualized as a system of (1) removing the egg, (2) substituting the desired nucleus (perhaps large numbers of eggs and nuclei, thus producing large numbers of individuals with exactly the same characteristics), (3) culturing the new individuals in artificial uteri, (4) and then "harvesting" the new crop of identical human beings.[27]

The feasibility of making deliberate genetic changes and manufacturing people is potentially the most important concept to arise in the history of the human race. No other concept has greater long-range implications for the future of the species—it marks a turning point in the whole evolution of life. Even in the ancient myths man was constrained by his essence. He could not rise above his destiny. Today we can envision that change and choice.[28] *But will this new creature, "the clone," be human, animal, or what?*

Tools of Their Tools?

C. S. Lewis, professor of Medieval and Renaissance Literature at Cambridge University until his death in 1963, observed that "each new power won by man is a power over man as well." Certainly genetic design would be such a power; even though its medical aim were only to gain control over the basic "stuff" of our human constitution, it could no doubt also be turned into an instrument of political power, with or without the reinforcement of Huxley's imaginary "soma." Is it possible, echoing Henry David Thoreau, that men have become the tools of their tools?[29]

The biological time bomb pushes us to the edges of life, death, and humanity. Beauty and the beast—which will it be?

Here comes a candle to light you to bed,
Here comes a chopper to chop off your head.
Oranges and Lemons

4

It's All in Your Head: The Psychological Time Bomb

DURING A COUNSELING SESSION, the psychologist showed Harry an inkblot and asked him what he saw. "Sex!" The psychologist then pulled out another inkblot and laid it over the first one. "And what do you see this time, Harry?" "Sex," replied Harry, giving the picture a quick glance. Once again the psychologist placed an inkblot in front of Harry. This time, before the psychologist had even opened his mouth, Harry blurted out, "Sex!" The psychologist shook his head, cleared his throat, and announced his diagnosis, "Harry, you have an extreme obsession with sex!" Harry retorted, "*I* have an extreme obsession with sex? *You* are the one who showed me all those dirty pictures!"

SYSTEMS AND MORE SYSTEMS

Active Analytic Psychotherapy
Analytic Group Therapy
Authoritarian Psychotherapy
Bibliotherapy
Client-centered Therapy
Conditioned-Reflex Therapy

66

Depth-Oriented Therapy
Didactic Group Therapy
Directive Psychotherapy
Experimental Therapy
Family Therapy
General Semantics
Gestalt Therapy
Group-centered Therapy
Group Psychotherapy
Hypnotherapy
I.D. Level Therapy
Learning Theory Therapy
Logotherapy
Multiple Therapy
Nondirective Therapy
Objective Psychotherapy
Orgare Therapy
Psychoanalytically Oriented Psychotherapy
Psychobiologic Psychotherapy
Psychodrama
Psychotherapy
Psychotherapy by Reciprocal Inhibition
Rational Psychotherapy
Reconstructive Therapy
Re-Educative Therapy
Round-Table Psychotherapy
Sector Therapy
Vegetotherapy
Will Therapy

The psychological time bomb is filled with voices expressing answers to the needs and problems of people. Most of these voices agree that "It's all in your head." The disagreement is over what the "all" in your head is! How can it be discovered? Where should it be directed? What distinguishes good behavior? Who's offering any answers? Let's listen to a few of the louder voices in all these systems in order to answer that last question and get a handle on the psychological time bomb.

Freud—The Pleasure Seeker

Sigmund Freud has been discussed and cussed more than any other person in the psychological field. The three most popular contributions of his work have been the concepts of the subconscious, free association, and the Freudian slip.

Although there were writers who preceded Freud in pointing out the existence of the unconscious, no one, either before or after, has exceeded him in the penetrating originality and rich detail with which he described unconscious psychic phenomena. Unconscious activity, said Freud, is the true instinctive molder of human destiny, and it is a boiling reservoir of unfulfilled sexual desires accumulated from infancy.[1]

In the late 1890s Freud developed his exploratory method of free association, which then became the basic tool of his psychoanalysis. The patient reclined on the couch, and the analyst sat down behind the patient's head. In free association the patient was instructed to let his mental processes go, with as little conscious direction as possible, and to tell the analyst everything that passed through his mind, no matter how trivial, irrelevant, disconnected, or unpleasant. Hopefully, in this way the patient would present the analyst with clues which could lead to the unconscious roots of his difficulties.[2]

The Freudian slip is the most frequently used concept—usually in a joking way—by the man on the street. To Freud, slips of the tongue, pen, and memory, and many of the daily mishaps that we call "accidents" are not meaningless errors but unconscious revelations of desires or wishes. The man who forgets to buy a present for his wife on their anniversary or to introduce her at a social gathering is not "absent-minded." He is expressing his unconscious feelings. Underlying feelings, wishes or desires are invariably of a sexual nature striving for personal satisfaction.[3] *Human behavior is motivated by pleasure!*

Adler—The Power Seeker

A succession of schisms occurred in the analytic movement through six of Freud's pupils. Alfred Adler, the first to break with Freud, felt that a person's development was conditioned by his social environment, rather than by biological forces, and he insisted that an individual could be analyzed and understood in terms of his present purposes or life goals rather than in terms of his infantile past.[4]

Adler developed a system in individual psychology based on the contention that emotional disturbances arise from feelings of inferiority and represent an individual's striving for power. *Instead of sex, human behavior is motivated by power!*

Jung—The Mystical Purpose Seeker

Carl Jung's rebellion from Freud's causative theory and practice led him to a purposeful and goal-striving interpretation of behavior. However, his thoughts were often confusing and complicated, to the point of being mystical, and his collective life purposes were criticized for being vague and nontestable.

His system has the quality of an esoteric religion, and at times it seems to take the patient away from reality and encourage the development of a mystical fantasy life. *Human behavior is motivated by subjective, somewhat mystical purposes!*[6]

Frankl—The Meaning Seeker

Viktor Frankl is the leader and originator of the school of logotherapy or existential analysis. He developed his therapy during the three grim years he spent in Auschwitz and other Nazi prisons. When he gained his freedom he learned that almost his entire family had been wiped out through those incredible years of suffering and degradation.

Frankl believes a person can discover meaning in life three ways: (1) by doing a deed; (2) experiencing a value; or (3) by suffering. *Instead of pleasure (Freud) or power (Adler) human behavior is motivated by meaning.*[7]

Rogers—"Cure Yourself"

Carl Rogers was the originator and primary exponent of nondirective counseling or client-centered therapy. Because all the responsibility for the direction of therapy lies with the client, it's not necessary for the therapist to have any great knowledge of personality diagnosis or dynamics. The therapist takes no real responsibility for guidance of the disturbed client, but rather views him as an equal and therefore capable of "curing" himself. A better term for this kind of therapy is not counseling but active listening. *Human behavior is motivated by self preservation!*

Glasser—Three R's of Psychology

William Glasser's creation of Reality Therapy is not another modification or variant of Freudian analysis—it's absolutely antithetical. Glasser lists six postulates or presuppositions that are characteristic of simple counseling, from orthodox psychoanalysis to nondirective therapy. They are:

(1) the reality of mental illness
(2) reconstructive exploration of the patient's past
(3) transference
(4) an unconscious which must be explored
(5) interpretation rather than evaluation of behavior
(6) change through insight and permissiveness

Reality therapy challenges the validity of all six of these.

For Freud, the basic human needs, which are presumably unfulfilled in what Freud called the neurotic, are sex and aggression. For Glasser, the basic human needs are relatedness and respect, and a person can satisfy these needs by doing what is *realistic, responsible,* and *right.*[9]

Ellis—Talk Yourself to Health

Albert Ellis calls his system "rational psychotherapy." *Human emotion in the adult human being is primarily caused and controlled by thinking.* The disturbed individual has adopted irrational and illogical ideas that then cause him to behave in a neurotic or psychotic fashion.

A person can change the nature of his feelings from negative to positive by changing the internalized sentences, or self-talk, with which he created the feelings in the first place.[10]

Skinner—Utopian Box for Pigeons and People

B. F. Skinner is the most influential of living American psychologists, and the most controversial contemporary figure in the science of human behavior. He is adored as a messiah and abhorred as a menace. As leader of the "behavioristic" psychologists, who liken man to a machine, Skinner is vigorously opposed both by Freudian psychoanalysts and by humanists.

The psychological time bomb is filled with many conflicting voices of theory and practice which resound with fear and confusion. But more frightening and confusing than all the rest combined is the voice of B. F. Skinner.

In his latest book, *Beyond Freedom and Dignity,* Skinner proposed that man can no longer afford freedom, and therefore it must be replaced with control over both his conduct and his culture. Like the utopians who preceded him, Skinner envisions a society in which men of good will can work, love, and live in security and harmony. He wants enough to eat, a clean environment, and safety from nuclear catastrophe for all mankind.

Skinner believes that human behavior can be precisely predicted and shaped, just as though it were a chemical reaction. Central to his approach is a method of conditioning which has been used with uniform success on laboratory animals: giving rewards to mold the subject to the experimenter's will. According to Skinner and his followers, the same technique will work equally well with humans.[12]

Underlying his method is the Skinnerian conviction that behavior is determined not from within (as is believed by nonbehaviorists) but from without. "Unable to understand how or why the person we see behaves as he does, we attribute his behavior to a person inside," Skinner explains. Mistakenly, we believe that man "initiates, originates and creates, and in doing so he remains divine. We say that he is autonomous." Skinner insists that autonomy is a myth, and that belief in an "inner man" is a superstition that originates as does belief in God, in man's inability to understand his world. Skinner further believes that man no longer needs such fictions as "something going on inside the individual, states of mind, feelings, purposes, expectancies and all of that."[13]

The ultimate logical dilemma in Skinner's thinking is this: what are the sources for the standards of good and evil in his ideal society? Who decides what constitutes pleasure and pain or reward and punishment when man and his environment are limitlessly manipulated? This isn't so hard nor nearly so important when manipulating pigeons. *But pigeons are not people!*

TM=MT Your Head!

Another voice which makes up the psychological time bomb is TM—Transcendental Meditation—as taught by India's Maharishi Mahesh Yogi. People in every spectrum of society are beginning to practice TM as a means of mental and physical relaxation, stress relief, awareness, expansion, and "development to a fully evolved state of life." Housewives, businessmen, scientists, high-ranking military officers, prisoners, students, and even young children are meditating.

To gain a clear understanding of TM, we must initially look at Maharishi Mahesh Yogi, who has brought this technique of meditation to the west. Maharishi was born in India, graduated from Allahabad University with a physics degree, and thereafter became the favorite disciple of "His Divinity Swami Brahmananda Saraswati, Jagodguru, Bhagwan Shankaracharya of Jyotir Math," at that time one of India's four great leaders.

Just before Swami died, he commissioned Maharishi to evolve a simple form of meditation which could be learned and practiced by anyone. Maharishi consented, retreated to the Himalayan Mountains for two years, and then emerged with the yoga technique he called Transcendental Meditation.

When the people of Southern India were slow in accepting it, he decided to take it to the West, to the people "who are in the habit of accepting things quickly." He went first to London (where he achieved fame as the guru of the Beatles) and then came to America.[14] The claims made for TM are phenomenal! TM will "relieve stress and tension, improve physical and mental health, increase creativity, expand pure awareness, relax, expand your life, and grow to your full potential." "Find your way to the tranquillity of inner enlightenment."[15]

While TM is filtering into public education systems (under the name "The Science of Creative Intelligence"), military installations, and government offices, many are concerned that it is actually a systematic religious philosophy. *Psychology Today* wrote, "The Science of Creative Intelligence, as it is called, is clearly a revival of ancient Indian Brahmanism and Hinduism. Its origins lie in the ancient texts—Vedas, Upanishads, Bhagavad-Gita, the teachings of Buddha . . . ."[16] The *Los Angeles Times* said, "TM leaders conceded that the metaphysical base behind TM is a revival of ancient Brahmanism and Hinduism."[17]

To meditate transcendentally, it's necessary to empty your mind. Since most of us cannot afford that very often, we keep looking for another way to fill the visceral vacuum while continuing to run on our mental treadmills. Fortunately there is no lack of contemporary systems to choose from. There are encounter groups, seminars, ways of seeing, and so on, ad infinitum.

TA: I'm OK—You're OK—Sometimes

Transactional Analysis (TA) is a form of group psychotherapy. Originated by the late Eric Berne, it focuses attention on characteristic interactions between individuals and the "games" they play in social situations. In his book, *Games People Play*, Berne attempted to describe the most common games. To dramatize them, and demonstrate their relevance to everyday life, he gives each one a colloquial label and exposes its true purpose as either a "con," a "gimmick," or a "payoff" —that is, a deceptive trick, an ulterior motive, or a reward of some kind. In the "yes, but" game, for example, a woman courts a compliment but then acts as though it was unde-

74 □ *The Detonation of Time Bombs*

served once it's given. In this way she is attempting to demonstrate her superiority by making the complimenter feel stupid. That's the "pay-off" which he has been "conned" into making. Other game titles are "Rapo," "Let's You and Him Fight," and "Ain't It Awful."[18]

In Berne's own language, a game is "a recurring series of transactions, often repetitive, superficially rational¯ with a concealed motivation." He held that each of these games is by itself merely a segment of a 'script' which a person uses in "performing" throughout life. When this script is analyzed, it is found to be an unconscious plan based on fantasies derived from early experience, and a major force in shaping the individual's entire life. TA has therefore been described by Berne as the analyses of scripts.[19]

In TA the personality is arbitrarily divided into three parts: parent, adult, and child. A shorthand, rhythmic explanation is that the "parent" part is concerned with what you were taught; the "adult" part with what you think; the "child" part with what you feel. TA is a concrete system for looking at oneself. It is widely used in therapy and in business to help people clarify their thinking and feelings, and then change their behavior.

TA has experienced an even greater penetration of the masses than TM. There is now TA for business, TA for parents, TA for teens and even TA for tots! Its popularity is due primarily to its simplistic description of the relationship dynamics of people on every level.

You Are What You Est!

Est works! At least that's what *est* graduates all over America are eagerly telling their friends, families, co-workers, and just about anyone else who will listen. Thousands have taken the *est* training—including such celebrities as John Denver, Valerie Harper, Cloris Leachman, Joanne Woodward, Yoko Ono, and Jerry Rubin—with incredible results!

Est has two meanings. It is the Latin word for "it is," and also an acronyn whose initials stand for Erhard Seminars Training, named after its creator, Werner Erhard. People are flocking to this 60-hour experience: young and old, confident and confused, divorced and married, professionals, housewives, students, rich, and not so rich (but rarely poor). The reason for est's following is that even though most of the people who go are doing well, their lives aren't really satisfying; in *est* talk, trying to make their lives satisfying wasn't satisfying either.[20]

Most disciplines have a basic content and specific techniques to help get it across. They want to share certain thoughts and ideas that they think are worthwhile. *Est* has no thoughts or ideas that they think are worthwhile. *Est* deals only with the context in which these things are held—it does not deal with content.

Erhard says, "The *est* training is about aliveness, satisfaction, fulfillment and the experience of completion. Whatever *est* is about lies within you, not within me. In the training, we present what we call 'space.' Space, in our terminology, is an opportunity for you to discover what *your* experience is with respect to some part of life. *The aim of the est training is a practically oriented philosophical education that is experienced rather than believed.*" To experience your life is to *est*; to *est* is to "get it."

Most criticisms of *est* come from one of four points of view: (1) that it is fascistic, (2) that it is brainwashing, (3) that it is too abbreviated to have any long-term or significant effect, and (4) that it is narcissistic.[21] Whatever the criticism, most of the *est* graduates seem to "get it."

Lifespring—Wound Loosely!

Like *est*, Lifespring training is out to create an environment where you can alter the way you see yourself and the world in order to experience more joy and fulfillment in life. The results achieved depend on each individual's experience of the training rather than the intellectual content and mechanics of it. You may not be able to explain it, but what you will *know* is that it *worked!* (i.e., you got it!)

Unlike *est*, which claims not to be a religion, therapy encounter, or psychology, Lifespring is a blend of various approaches found today in the human potential movement. Some of the experience areas of the people who developed the training are meditation, gestalt psychology, Zen, human relations training, mind power methods, and transpersonal psychology.

The training is rooted in humanistic psychology which is based on the assumption that people already have the knowledge, creativity, and vitality they need for personal fulfillment. The most common feedback centers on an expansion of self-confidence, heightened feelings of self-worth and the development of warmer and more sensitive relationships. All of this is discovered in a comfortable setting with a casual atmosphere.

John Hanley, founder of Lifespring, expresses the problem many people face in this way: "To the degree your life takes effort, is to the degree it's not working."

What or Who Is Man?

The systems and more systems of psychology offer a flood of various voices filled with answers for man's needs. But the bottom-line consideration in each system comes down to the nature of man.

Who or what is man: an animal? a machine? an energy? or perhaps a god?

Whatever the answer to this question, it must be true to life as it is and people as they are! Without an adequate answer to this final question all the therapies in the world can only assist you in firmly planting your feet—in midair!

Goosey goosey gander
Whither shall I wander?
Upstairs and downstairs,
And in my lady's chamber;
There I met an old man who wouldn't say his prayers;
I took him by the left leg,
And threw him down the stairs.

Goosey Goosey Gander

5

Heaven Help Us!
The Religious Time Bomb

IT WAS A COOL, CRISP Saturday afternoon and Mr. Marshall was busily installing a new television antenna on his roof. He was just about through, and hurrying to finish before the football game came on, when he slipped and began to fall. He slid down the roof, over the edge, and barely caught himself on the gutter. There he was dangling by his fingertips, two stories above the ground, "Is there anybody down there who can help me?" Not a soul heard him in his desperate moment.

With no time to wait around for a response, he then looked up and yelled out, "Is there anybody up there who can help me?" At that precise instant, the clouds parted and a voice blared out, "*BELIEVE AND LET GO!*" In a total panic Mr. Marshall quickly glanced down again and then back up and shouted, "Is there anybody *else* up there who can help me?"

The religious time bomb, like the psychological, is exploding with a barrage of various answers to man's problem. But for most people, all it is offering them in their desperation is a leap in the dark. *Believe and let go!*

Contemporary Cults

In the mid-1960s there were an estimated 1500 religions, both old and new, in California alone, and that number has

77

continued to increase and enlarge its following. Although the soil for the growth of religious cults seems to be particularly fertile on the West Coast and in the metropolitan East, they have sprouted up everywhere. Some of them are grotesque, some sinister, and others naive, yet their attraction holds. With hungry hearts young adherents come to them searching for something or Someone to reconcile their alienation and make sense out of their chaos.[1]

To get a basic grasp of the many religious cults, let's briefly survey a few of the more popular ones: two "missions," two "mystics," two "families," and two "churches"!

Today, informed estimates put the number of recently organized cults anywhere from 2500 to as high as 5000, most with only a handful of members. The largest have hundreds of thousands of followers, often living in communes or colonies and making forays onto college campuses and into the streets to garner converts. In the past, it's been easy for most people to brush the various cults aside, but the tragedy of the mass murder-suicide of the People's Temple has forced the issue to the forefront. The Rev. Jim Jones, who had been honored and praised for his efforts to help humanity, led 910 followers into a paranoid suicide pact in the steamy jungle of Guyana at a cult compound called Jonestown. It's one thing to capture a person's mind, but to kill a person is intolerable!

MISSIONS

Scientology: Science Fiction Religion?

Scientology is a contemporary western religion, founded and directed by the science-fiction writer L. Ron Hubbard. In 1949, whether knowingly or not, he predicted his own future in a jocular speech to a convention of fellow authors: "Writing for a penny a word is ridiculous. If a man really wanted to make a million dollars, the best way would be to start his own religion."[2]

The next year Hubbard put his prediction in print with *Dianetics: The Modern Science of Mental Health,* which expounded his psychological theories and later became Scientology's scripture. The original intent of dianetics was secular, but subsequent to its publication, Hubbard "discovered" the existence of the soul or, in his terminology, the Thetan, the conscious being that inhabits the human body.

Embroidering on Hinduism and Buddhism, Hubbard announced that Thetans are reincarnated over trillions of years. For Scientologists, truth became stranger than science fiction. An example is Hubbard's explanation of why someone might have difficulty crying: "He was once a primordial clam whose water ducts had been clogged with sand." [3]

In 1976 Scientologists claimed an organization of more than 3 million members, 26 churches and 120 missions in the United States alone, along with still many more world-wide. They are supported by church members, who pay established "donations" ($25 to $750) for counseling sessions, the sale of church literature, and by payments received for advanced courses in church philosophy and specialized training. The total the church items "clear" can range between $1000 and $5000 (per year—per member). And sometimes more! [4]

In 1965 a blistering report was published by a governmental board of inquiry in Australia. Their report stated that while claiming to be the world's largest mental health organization, the Hubbard Association of Scientologists International is "the world's largest organization of unqualified persons engaged in the practice of dangerous techniques which masquerade as mental therapy." [5]

Divine Light Mission: Teenage Guru

Formed in 1970 by the then thirteen-year-old Maharaj Ji, the Divine Light Mission has weathered a financial crisis, a family battle for control, and slackening membership figures. Considered by his premies (devotees) to be the "Savior of Mankind," Maharaj Ji calls himself a Perfect Master. According to the Indian youth there is only one such human being on earth at a time (his own late father and Jesus were also perfect masters), and they alone have the ability to teach that which is perfect—the knowledge of God. [6]

In 1974 Maharaj Ji numbered his followers at over 50,000

in the United States and 30 million more around the world. In the last few years he has matured and changed his life style considerably. He no longer shoots his followers with a water pistol or makes gadget-grabbing shopping trips!

East and West clearly mix as the message of Maharaj Ji's mission is unravelled. By giving himself to the Guru, a follower is plugged into the true source of the "divine energy" flow, and his mind is automatically emptied of all its troubles and pressures by the Perfect Master's divine knowledge. In the Divine Light Mission a person doesn't need his mind anyway, because according to Maharaj Ji the "illusion" of individuality is precisely what causes the evil a person experiences in the first place. It sounds good, but is peace at the price of being a nonperson worth it?

MYSTICS

Krishna Consciousness: Chanting to Semi-Consciousness!

The International Society of Krishna-Consciousness (ISKCON) has only been active in the U.S. for 12 years, but during that time it has attracted an estimated 5000 young Americans in at least 30 cities. ISKCON was introduced here in 1965 by its founder and leader, His Divine Grace A.C. Bhaktivedanta Swami Prabhupada, a small, bald, stone-faced 81-year-old Bengali.

His disciples believe Prabhupada is the latest in a long line of divine reincarnations that can be traced back 5000 years to the first appearance of Lord Krishna (the principle incarnation of Vishnu—the second member of the Hindu trinity).[7]

With their heads shaved and pigtailed and clothed in saffron robes, members of ISKCON have become a familiar sight on college campuses and in major metropolitan areas. They dance down sidewalks and on street corners, beating their drums, clinking finger-cymbals, shaking rattles, and chanting the Hare Krishna mantra, "Hare Krishna Rama Rama" (the minimum obligation is to chant 1728 repetitions a day). Some people only stare at them or ridicule, some are enticed to listen, and others are angered, having lost family or friends to their ranks.[8]

The Krishnas believe that their ritual chanting, along with incredibly severe programs of self-denial and absolute obedience, will help liberate them from the endless mortal cycle of aging, disease, death, and rebirth—and earn them an eternal place with Lord Krishna in Nirvana where the cycle of reincarnation has ceased.[9]

Chanting is one of the most important rituals of the ISKCON liturgy. It is also the most familiar aspect of the Krishna movement and the origin of its popular name Hare Krishna. According to the Krishna consciousness movement, the Vedic scriptures (the old sacred writings of Hinduism) recommend constantly chanting the name of God in order to develop a love of Krishna and attain salvation through union with him.[10]

Professional observers, like Dr. William J. Winter, former professor of neuropathology at the University of Miami, say that this relentless chanting assaults the limbic-hypothalamic-reticular activating systems of the Krishnas' brains and deteriorates their capacity for objective discriminatory thinking, thus reducing them to zombies. Krishna Consciousness may be the ultimate wipeout in the religious time bomb![11]

Zen Buddhism: Teach Me about Nothing!

If you really want to know what Zen Buddhism is all about, don't ask a Zen Master. One old Master, whenever he was asked to explain Zen Buddhism, merely lifted one of his fingers. He didn't say a thing! In response to the same question, another Master kicked a ball; a third slapped his inquirer in the face. With these kinds of answers it is difficult, if not impossible, to understand Zen. It's definitely a mystical experience![12]

In his book, *Religions of Man*, Dr. Huston Smith wrote: "Entering the Zen outlook is like stepping through Alice's looking glass. One finds oneself in a topsy-turvy wonderland in which everything seems quite mad—charmingly mad for the most part—but mad all the same. It is a world of bewildering dialogues, obscure conundrums, stunning paradoxes, flagrant contributions, and abrupt non-sequiters, all carried off in the most urbane, cheerful, and innocent style." [13]

In 1959 the Japanese roshi (headmaster) Shunryu Suzuki, now in his seventies, arrived in the U.S. and became the priest of this country's first Zen Buddhist congregation in San Francisco. Short, slight, and possessing a good sense of humor, Suzuki Roshi, as he is often called, now devotes all his time to Zen students at a monastery in Tossajara (150 miles south of San Francisco). He is dedicated to teaching his students how to find the answers of life within themselves. [14]

Zen Buddhism consists of three keys. The first is to "sit and meditate" (zazen). The second key is the content of meditation. Called a *koan*, it is a blatantly absurd statement, for example, "What is the sound of one hand clapping?" Since the *koan* cannot be logically resolved, the third key—*satori*—has to follow. *Satori* is an immediate experience of truth but without an understanding of what truth is. Suddenly, you have surpassed thinking and are simply experiencing. No longer locked in the closet of your own reason, you are now free to burst into the sunlight of total Enlightenment. [15]

Zen Buddhism can be summed up in the Zen poem entitled "Trust in the Heart":

> If you want the truth to stand clear before you,
> Never be for or against.
> The struggle between "for" and "against"
> Is the mind's worst disease.

Years ago in Washington, D.C. a Zen Buddhist devotee made a statement to me that seemed to clearly capture what it's all about. He said, "I owe everything to my teacher because he taught me nothing!"

FAMILIES

Children of God: Happy Hookers for Jesus?

After a stormy and unsuccessful career in the established church, David Brandt Berg arrived in Huntington Beach,

California at the peak of the Jesus Movement in 1968. There he assembled a small group of disciples around him, the leading members of which were his own children, Faith, Aaron, Jonathan and Deborah. He called himself Moses David, and considered himself a prophet and king.

Teaching a fundamentalist forsake-all gospel, they advocated the adoption of a community, or colony, life style. Dubbed the "children of doom," and dedicated to their beliefs, they set out to convince America of her future judgment, the futility of her churches, and an impending communist invasion. Their strong conviction of these unusual claims, together with their public demonstrations of song, dance, and doom threats, attracted the attention of the church, the media, and eventually the law. They were soon receiving strong criticism.

However, this was just what the Children of God expected. They had been taught that the "System" was devilish and controlled by the anti-Christ. Their enemy, they were told, would persecute, defame, and slander them, call their leader a false prophet, and eventually force them to go "underground." They would then keep their precious doctrines and the true nature of their life style a secret from the "evil and deluded" outside world.

Giving their lives and possessions for the gospel's sake, dropouts, ex-junkies, and young adults in emotional turmoil were among those drawn into this exclusive group. By February 1975, their paper, "Nation News," was claiming totals of 272,693 converts, 179,605 baptisms and 6,698 new full-time workers since October 1971. However, recent estimates of their present numbers indicate a total of only 4000 adults, living in 400 different colonies situated in 65 countries around the world.[16]

Moses David, now fifty-eight, has gone into seclusion over the past few years. He continues to carry on his role of latter-day prophet (Moses) and King of Israel (David) by writing a profusion of "MO" letters—more than 500 in five years. He mails these to his colonies to be printed and distributed on street corners in exchange for donations. His letters, he insists, are "God's Word for today" and they have supplanted the biblical Scriptures (God's Word for yesterday).[17]

One of the most shocking MO letters encouraged the female children of God to become "Happy Hookers for Jesus." Berg, who is said to have several concubines, was even photographed by *Time* magazine with more than a dozen of his "Happy Hookers" in the Canary Islands.

Another shocking MO letter is entitled "God Bless You—And Good-Bye!" In this letter, Moses David confesses he has been a "false prophet who passed off his own thoughts as divinely inspired," and "led you by your faith in Jesus into the darkness of my mind." The movement, he announces, "has come to an end now and forever." However, the Children of God are far from disbanding. They argue that the letter is a fraud. Later Moses David made a tape denying the MO letter confessional as a "demented hoax."[18] It takes one to call one?!

Love Israel: The Church of Armageddon

The Church of Armageddon is a religious sect led by the undisputed dictator Love Israel. Hence the name Love Israel or Love Family.

When a person joins Love Israel, he or she gives up any "Christian" identity. Everyone takes the last name of Israel and virtuous first names, such as Serenity, Charity, Serious, Trust, and so on. They are issued identification by the church with statistics converted to cubits and stones. Followers are told they are the Children of God and the Virgin Mary, and their date of birth becomes the day they joined the sect. They reside in immaculately kept houses in the Seattle area and live a commune-type farm life.

All the property of new members is turned over to the church and either put to use by the family or disposed of. This, along with all financial decisions, is at the discretion of Love Israel. No one in the commune except Love is allowed to handle money. Only Love and four elders are permitted to operate a vehicle, and the list of restrictions goes on and on.

Three deaths have occurred in the Love family. The first two members died of acute toluene intoxication. The industrial solvent was allegedly inhaled while being used in some sort of religious rite. The official cause of death was listed as "accident." Because toluene isn't considered to be a controlled substance, no apparent violation of the law took place and no criminal action was initiated. The third death occurred when one of the family members fell out of a tree. The official cause of that death was also listed as "accident."

The Love Israel Family is dedicated to helping those who suffer from loneliness, misunderstanding, and limiting false beliefs. The methods they use to help people through their problems are the Bible, meditation, chanting, chemicals, or any other means God reveals to them.

CHURCHES

The Local Church: Out of Shout—Out of Mind

In 1962 Witness Lee, minister from Taiwan, came to the United States to settle in Los Angeles. There he established a church of his teachings and from that point on it was known as the Local Church. In the late 1960s, about seventy of his followers emigrated to Houston. Others then moved to Seattle, Chicago, Akron, and Atlanta and by 1974 there were about fifty Local Churches in the U.S.

The most striking thing about the Local Church is its suppression of individuality. They teach that the only thing God cares about is himself. People are of value to him only in so far as they can be "mingled" with him. Therefore, "human nature" is to be despised and "burned away." Their teaching effectively conveys that God isn't interested in the individual and his ability to think and reason. God doesn't work through the human mind, and he doesn't want the individual to use it. True spirituality involves "getting out of your mind."

Part of the process of working-out one's salvation in the Local Church involves "killing" the person's old world, all the old attachments and the old self that went with them, especially the individual emotional and intellectual life. All of these things stand in the way of the release of the spirit and must therefore be removed.

The process by which a person's old self is "killed" is a major spiritual practice of the Local Church—"pray-reading." It consists of an insistently repetitious shouting of scriptural phrases while punctuating them with even louder Amen's, Hallelujah's or Lord Jesus's. Pray-reading the Bible exercises the spirit and does not give the mind time to work. Shout it out—of your mind!

Unification Church: The Moonies Are Out in Full

Sun Myung Moon launched the Unification Church in 1954 in Seoul, Korea, and three years later published his book, *Divine Principle,* the new revelation he claimed to have received from God.

According to Moon, Jesus Christ appeared to him on a Korean hillside in 1936—when Moon was sixteen—and gave him the "key to righteousness and restoration of the Kingdom of Heaven on Earth." The task had originally been given to Adam and Christ but, Moon says, both of them failed miserably. Now only Moon possesses the key which can decode the Bible's truth, and he is therefore only carrying out his God-given task.

On January 1, 1972, Moon says God told him to go to America. During 1973 and 1974 Moon conducted marathon speaking tours throughout the U.S. and attracted many followers. "I will conquer and subjugate the world," he said. "I am your brain." The latter statement has become literal truth for a growing coterie of young American converts, who regard the South Korean cult leader as the second Christ. Asking no questions, they obediently hawk candy and flowers, raising millions to spread the faith. They exist on a shoestring, while Moon lives in lordly fashion in his 25-room mansion in New York's Westchester County.[19]

In 1975 the Unification Church's national budget alone was $11 million, not counting the expenses of 120 local branches and affiliates. As the cult steadily grows, all those involved believe that a "Lord of the Second Advent" (Moon, though this is not stated publicly) will physically redeem mankind by fathering a perfect family. The Unification Church is actually a blend of Christian terminology, occultism, and dualism.[20]

As in most of the cults considered in the religious time bomb, one of the greatest concerns is the kidnaping of vulnerable young people. Parents have reacted angrily and desperately against the "mind control" techniques used to capture their children. In many of these cults the members are used as a kind of "slave labor" force to make money for the head or heads of the mission, mystic, family or church.

Contemporary Religious Systems

No matter what flavor of religion you chose in the U.S., most of them taste alike. Catholic, Protestant, Jew, and all their various spinoffs only seem to be offering more leaps in the dark.

Man-Made Religion

When a man makes his own religion he is attempting to relate to God through a system of do's and don't's and limiting the whole process to himself. It's like trying to climb up to heaven on a six-foot ladder—it just doesn't reach very far!

Man-made religion is filled with existential humanism (the man-does-it-all extreme) at one end of the spectrum and mysticism (the God-does-it-all extreme) at the other. Both ends are saturated with God-words without substance and experiences without a logical basis.

First a boy believes in Santa Claus, then he doesn't believe in Santa Claus, and finally he believes he *is* Santa Claus! The existential humanist's approach to God is similar. He believes in God first, then he doesn't believe in God, and finally he believes he is God!

At the other end of the spectrum the mystics are looking for God to speak to them, lead them, or demonstrate himself to them at each and every turn! The problem here is to be able to discern when it's God's voice, leading or demonstrating and when it's only their own or someone else's voice.

Stained-Glass Voice

In order for man-made religion to feel religious at either end of the spectrum, the atmosphere must be right. Whether it's a formal or informal setting the stained-glass voice always contributes to the religious tone. It also helps to have some-one who can go down deep and stay down long without com-ing up for air to deliver the sermon. That way people get ex-cited and emotionally hyped up about their religion, at least until they get to the parking lot. It doesn't have to say any-thing or make sense. It just has to feel good and sound spiri-tual!

As I was growing up, I asked around to find out how I could get my ticket to heaven. No sooner had I asked than I was presented with a list of twelve things I wasn't allowed to do. In looking over the list, I realized some of them were my fav-orite things and some were even my goals in life! Then I asked for the list of things I was allowed to do and still get my ticket. There were only four things on that list and all of them were weekly meetings to attend! I quickly saw that religion was basically a system of do's and don'ts—mostly don'ts—and that spelled nothing but drudgery!

The more closely the religious time bomb is examined the more you get the feeling that we may not be alone in our confusion. Imagine that all the religious leaders of both cult and man-made flavors were gathered before God in heaven. God looked out among them and inquired, "Who do you say I am?" One by one they each responded with their names and descriptions of him: "The Thetan of Thetans! The Source of Divine Energy! The Essence of All Consciousness! The Wholly Other! The Ground of Being! The Infinite Transcendent Em-anation!" and so on, ad infinitum. Finally, after the last one was finished, God rubbed his chin and muttered a puzzled, "Huh???"

Old Mother Goose,
When she wanted to wander,
Would ride through the air
On a very fine gander.
Old Mother Goose

6

The Twilight Zone:
The Parapsychological
Time Bomb

HAVING SPOKEN ON A UNIVERSITY campus in the Southwest, I
encountered some strange reverberations. A few days later a
student government leader called me late one evening in a
panic. "Tim, I've got to talk to you tonight!" he blurted out. I
met him at the student center just as soon as I could get there.
Fidgeting nervously, he related an incredible story. He had
just attended a seance where he had encountered the spirit
world face to face. He was obsessed by the voices he had heard
at the meeting, and was he scared!! When he finished his tale,
so was I! His experience didn't seem to be a trick. There was
something strangely real about it.

Next a girl called. Her roommate was a white witch who
had read her future from tarot cards. She had told her a young
man would come into her life and bring her good fortune. Several nights after this prediction, a fiery ball appeared to her
while she was in a meditative state. Then the fiery ball communicated that it had come to fulfill the prophecy. (It's one
thing for a fiery ball to appear, but it's quite another when
the fiery ball speaks!) Screaming, she ran from the room in
terror, afraid to tell anyone what had happened. The following night the fire returned. Now she was calling for help!

Last December an astrological counselor charted the next year's happenings for a friend of mine and his family. To date everything the counselor projected has occurred on schedule: intense marital problems in February, the husband would make a significant change in employment, and the wife would have an extremely serious health problem in the last week of October.

A college girl in Washington, D.C. slipped one morning and fell down a short flight of marble stairs. She dislocated her coccyx, but though in pain did not call her parents in New York City. No use worrying them she thought. She could manage by herself.

That evening her mother called. "What happened," her mother asked, "and how badly are you hurt?" Playing dumb, the girl asked why she had called.

"I had a dream last night," her mother replied. "I saw you fall off a ladder and hurt your back."

Even though the dream occurred before the fall, and it involved a ladder instead of a flight of stairs, still the girl could not believe it was all just a coincidence. She wondered if her mother's dream could have somehow been connected with her fall.[1]

What about these experiences? Are they coincidences? Are they imagination? Are they good or evil? Are they caused by an unknown power within man's psyche or by a group of spirits floating freely throughout the universe? What is life all about in the twilight zone?

Natural vs. Supernatural

There are two approaches to the twilight zone that compose the parapsychological time bomb. The "natural" scientific field of study and the "supernatural" occultic field of study.

SCIENTIFIC FIELD—NATURAL

In the 1930s experimentation with psychic phenomena developed into the field now known as parapsychology, a name selected to show that the field is both like and unlike that of psychology. The name was first used publicly in 1935 when a laboratory for studying psychic powers was established at Duke University in Durham, North Carolina. It's now the Institute for Parapsychology under the Foundation for Research on the Nature of Man.[2]

The first task of the Institute was to gather the basic research necessary to find out whether or not psychic phenomena were real. If no trace of psychic ability could be found when properly controlled experiments were made, then it was time the old question was settled once and for all and the world informed that there was no such thing. If, on the other hand, evidence of any extrasensory kind of abilities was obtained, it would mean that the nature of man potentially includes more than is normally experienced.

From the natural approach, parapsychology is an attempt to find out the facts about a definite class of phenomena by carefully controlled experimentation. It is striving to establish its respectability and respective domain just as the older sciences of physics, chemistry, biology, and psychology, and so on have already done.[3]

psi Ability

Parapsychology in the scientific field studies the mental abilities of ESP (extrasensory perception—sending and receiving mental messages) and PK (psychokinesis—moving objects by mental processes). Having obtained evidence of both ESP and PK, an English psychologist, Dr. Robert Thorless, suggested giving the abilities the combined name of the Greek letter *psi*. It doesn't even give a hint of their nature and yet it identifies them.[4]

One of the first objectives in researching the *psi* ability was to classify the various ways it came to a person's conscious attention. It turned out that in spite of what first seemed to be endless differences, most of the variations were superficial, and the cases actually took one of only about five different forms. Four of them involved ESP and the other one PK: (1) an hallucination (usually a visual one, but sometimes an auditory one); (2) an intuition; (3) a realistic dream; (4) an unrealistic or fantasy dream; and (5) the PK form.[5]

ESP—Communicating in the Sixth Sense

Extrasensory perception (ESP) is a response to someone or something possibly not perceivable to any known sense.[6] Apparently it's something that is unconscious. The person doesn't know when he will do it or how he does it, so he can't control it. Although some will do it more often or more accurately than others, the scientific field of study generally accepts that everyone has the ability.

Walls and barriers don't interfere with the extrasensory way of knowing and it's not limited by distance or time. Telepathy, clairvoyance, and precognition bring information from different parts of the world and different periods of time. But no matter where it comes from or what time it comes from, the method by which it comes is the same—it's ESP!

Communication from one living mind to another, the process called "telepathy," had often been reported, but for a long time no one knew whether or not that was actually what was happening. In the late 1920s and early 1930s the researchers were determined to find out.

Dr. Charles Richet, a French physiologist and Nobel Prize winner, made some careful experiments. He found that a person could sometimes draw a picture to match one unknown to anyone and hidden somewhere in an opaque envelope. This could not be telepathy (communication) because there was no one the person could have communicated with. Richet called it a sixth sense, and eventually it came to be known as clairvoyance (the power to perceive things outside the range of the natural senses).[9]

"Precognition," another word for prophecy, has also been established by extensive research as a scientific fact. Over many years and countless trials, the results have shown that subjects can, to a significant degree, foresee *before* shuffling a deck of cards what their order will be *after* they have been shuffled. After the precognition experiments had sufficiently demonstrated that ESP can go into the future, it was recognized that precognition and clairvoyance were almost the same thing. The only difference being one knew what something was in the present, and the other what it would be in the future. In most of the tests the future was only a few minutes away, but some of the tests did cover a longer period of time.[10]

PK—Moving Mountains?

The effect of mind over matter and the amount of evidence gathered in support of it is now so strong that no further proof of PK (Psychokinesis) is necessary.[11] PK occurs when the energy of the mind, usually contained in the brain and channeled to a function of the body, transcends the brain and affects things outside the body. In laboratory situations, the roll of a die or the needle of a PK machine are most commonly used to test this effect.[4] In daily life, it could go from the mind of the person and affect any object: a radio, a picture, a door, or possibly a table in a seance room.[12]

Mr. Nigel Richmond did some experimenting with the effect of thought on living organism, but instead of using plants, which had been done in the past, Richmond chose paramecia (a genus of single-celled animal organisms) for his experiment. He put a drop of water on a slide under a microscope, centered one animal under the cross-hairs, and then willed it to move in a certain direction, according to a random selection of targets. He did an extensive number of such tests, and his results showed that the tiny animals had responded in a manner which strongly suggested his thought had affected them.

A teacher in an English boys' school, John Randall, decided to use wood lice for his experimental animal. (They are commonly found in dark crevices and under rocks in dark, damp places.) In the test a wood louse was put into a small dish, and was placed over the center of a large cardboard diagram divided like a pie into five equal sectors. A single electric bulb, the only light in the room, was positioned directly above the dish, and when it was turned on, the louse would immediately try to get out of the lighted dish. Randall then tried to will the louse to crawl out onto the sector of the diagram he had chosen as the target.

The result was the animals went to the target sector, rather than to any of the others, a marginally significant number of times. As in the test with the paramecia, the human subjects definitely had an effect on the animals.[13]

PK—Thinking Your Way to Health?

Dr. Jean Barry, a physician, was interested to learn if the growth of harmful organisms, like certain disease-causing fungi, could be slowed down by human thought. By chance alone his results should have been about half hits and half misses, but instead, thirty-three of the thirty-nine tests completed were hits, only three were misses, and three were ties. The results definitely seemed to demonstrate something beyond mere chance. It appeared that his subjects had actually slowed down the growth of the fungus just by will power, indicating that the human mind—or some human minds—may indeed be able to exert an effect on living tissue.[14]

In ESP research what experiments can we believe, and whom can we trust? We can examine the experiment and the precautions taken to keep the participating subjects from cheating, but how do we know whether or not the experimenter is deliberately deceiving us? And in a world where people believe all kinds of nonsense, how can we be sure the experimenter isn't deceived himself?[15] However, what options are there?

The only stand science can take today for "uncaused" physical effects like these is that PK is real. The research that has been done does offer an explanation for it, and it certainly seems more rational than attributing it to a "boisterous" spirit."[16]

OCCULT FIELD—SUPERNATURAL

Operating from a natural base, the scientific field believes the only rational explanation for parapsychological phenomena is *psi* ability—ESP and PK. On the contrary, the occult field, operating from a supernatural base, believes a force outside man or even a "boisterous spirit" is a perfectly rational explanation as to the cause of parapsychological phenomena. The occult field can be divided into the three basic areas of *astrology, spiritualism,* and *witchcraft.*

Star Gazing—Not Just for Lovers

Astrology is the study of the positions and aspects of heavenly bodies with a view to predicting their influence on the course of human affairs. Llewellyn George, a prominent contemporary spokesman for astrology, defined it as "the study of life's reactions to planetary vibrations."[17]

The beginning of astrology dates back in ancient history as far as three millennia B.C. As far as we know, the Babylonians were the world's first astrologers. They erected towers called Ziggurats, in order to survey the heavens. Reaching some 270 feet high, these rested on top of a series of seven terraces, and were climbed by the ancient priests to reach the summit of the universe. These priests, who were the go-betweens for the king to the gods, surveyed the skies to discern the will of the deities. Although other ancient civilizations, the Chinese, Hindu, and Aztec, for instance, also had a form of astrology, it was the Babylonians who developed it into the form practiced today by the western world.[18]

Almost every major newspaper, besides the *Wall Street Journal,* carries its daily astrological column—at last count, more than 1200 across the United States. Some two million citizens are astrology addicts, requiring the services of an astrologer, while millions more are at least curious enough to purchase books and consult the newspaper astrology columns. Both *Horoscope* and *American Astrology* have a paid circulation of about a half million, and the field of astrology employs 12,000 full-time professionals and 175,000 part-time astrologers.[19]

It does seem ironic that astrology has risen so rapidly in our scientific age, but, as a young Japanese astrologer said, young people get interested in it because "they're trying to find their souls." The growing disillusionment with materialism has come at a time when science and technology have seemingly reached their zenith. Man has gone to the moon, but what does the moon mean to man? Astrology is an attempt to put meaning in the universe to make sense out of it.[20]

Spiritualism—Do Dead People Talk?

Spiritualism is the belief that the dead communicate with the living, usually through a medium. Spiritualism should not be confused with spiritism, which is the worship of spirits as practiced in many of the more primitive countries of the world. (For example, voodoo and black magic are both out-growths of spiritism.)

Only 150,000 Americans officially list Spiritualism as their religion, but a more accurate total of those who believe in it would probably be somewhere between 500,000 and 700,000. The Gallup polls have reported there are probably a million and a half to two million people in the world who believe man can communicate with the dead. More inflated figures in South America say that there are more than four million practicing spiritualists, three million in Brazil alone.[21]

Spiritualists say there are six different types of seances in which dead people communicate with the living: passivity, vocal reality, trumpet revelation, lights, transfiguration, and levitation. Many others scorn the sentimentalities of a seance but do try to discover a philosophy of the universe from the "advanced spirits." [22]

As spiritualism is examined, some of it must be ascribed to fakery and much of it to psychic phenomena, but there is still some of it that cannot be easily ascribed to anything but a supernatural source. That leaves the two other possibilities; either it comes from evil spirits or from the good spirits.[23]

Witchcraft—a Black and White Issue?

There are two kinds of witches, white witches and black witches. White witches use their power for good purposes; black witches for evil purposes. They both claim to be prac-ticing the oldest religion in the world—witchcraft.

By "old religion," witches mean that witchcraft is the original religion—going back long before Hinduism or the Old Testament origins of Christianity. Hans Holzer, a very sympathetic commentator on witchcraft, explains it like this: "The early religion of western and northern Europe was a nature religion in which the forces of the world around man were considered manifestations of divine power. In this respect, the early religion was pantheistic. . . . The image of the Mother Goddess, representing the forces in nature, developed and was eventually given a companion in the Horned God, representing the male principle. To the contemporaries of this civilization, the faith was simply 'religion,' but after the advent of Christianity it became known as the 'Old Religion' to emphasize the contrast."

The Horned God, the witches hasten to explain, isn't really Satan, even though he looks the part. He's probably Pan, they say, the Roman god of nature who was half god and half man. However, it would be easy to question that, considering they speak of him as Lucifer, a name given to Satan in the Bible and commonly used to refer to him.

A male witch is technically called a wizard, but most people today call him a warlock. All of the witches and warlocks are members of a *coven*—taken from the word *covenant*, meaning to come together.[24]

Members of a coven, usually thirteen in number—the priest or priestess, plus six men and six women—meet once a month on the night of the full moon. Their monthly meeting is called an esbat. In addition, there are eight sabbats: one at the beginning of each season, one for Halloween, one for the Maypole dance of May Eve, one on February Eve, and one on August Eve. The Bible of the Old Religion is called *The Book of Shadows*. It describes their rites, cures, charms, and spells and is read at every esbat and sabbat.[25]

In England there are 30,000 practicing witches. In Germany, according to the German Medical Information Service, 10,000 people are engaged in witchcraft, with the numbers increasing steadily over the last ten years.

In America, one member of the Old Religion says there are

nearly ten million practicing witches here. Of these, four million are officially registered with the witchcraft centers. Since the U.S. Census Bureau doesn't take a count of witches, it's hard to get accurate figures. Sybil Leek, a self-styled British witch as well as a medium, says the witch population has increased 40 percent in the past five years.[26]

Dr. John Charles Cooper, chairman of the department of philosophy at Eastern Kentucky University, wrote: "There is such a thing as witchcraft; it exists and it works. I have seen the fear that it inspires in college students enrolled in large universities, fear that passes over into clinical paranoia in some instances. And I have seen it work on white, middle-class, well-educated people in the heartland of the United States."[27]

The Twilight Zone—Scientific or Spooky?

The parapsychological time bomb is filled with the unknown. Can the strange experiences be explained by the scientific method or by the spooky occult—or is it a little of both?

A dillar, a dollar,
A *ten o'clock scholar*
What makes you come so soon?
You used to come at ten o'clock,
And now you come at noon.
A Dillar, a Dollar

7

Dick and Jane:
The Educational Time Bomb

DURING A DISCUSSION in a high school English class, the question of choosing colleges was brought up. One bright girl remarked, "Well, the first thing you have to decide is whether you want to go to a coeducational school or an educational one!" Nothing is easier in America than to attend college, and nothing is harder than to get educated!

No matter what approach is taken toward the issues of education, there isn't a whole lot there to be excited about. The educational time bomb is charged with problems: (1) *valueless education*—academics without values; (2) *educationless education*—training rather than educating; and (3) *instant and boundless education*—mediated learning and information bombardment.

The Boiling Pot of Education

In the 1960s Americans watched the rumblings of chaos and anarchy sweep the nation's colleges. In the 1970s the battleground has shifted down to the junior and senior high schools. William Waugh, the Associated Press education writer, puts it like this: "America's high schools—from the ghetto to the suburbs—are like boiling cauldrons. No one can predict when the pot will boil over, but already violence, vandalism, and noisy protest are common." [1]

James S. Coleman, Professor of Sociology at the University of Chicago, believes there are three key problems now facing the schools: One is the dissatisfaction of parents and students and the low morale among teachers because of their feeling that the schools are not working well. Second is the extreme loss of the schools' authority, particularly with regard to maintaining discipline. Third is the unsatisfactory level of academic achievement at schools everywhere—in small towns, big cities, and suburbs. [2]

Education—Boiling in the Big City

Nearly five million children in the U.S.—10 percent of its public school population—attend school in the classrooms of big cities, yet the education these children receive amounts to a national scandal. Their achievement levels are three, four, or even five years below the nationwide average. Their hallways are filled with drugs and violence; in 1978, cases of aggravated assault in schools topped 150,000, and vandalism cost city school districts an estimated $600 million. Truancy is so high that most attempts to curtail it have been dropped and dropping out completely has become all too common. Costs are soaring and because the cities can't pay the bills, school board after school board has been forced to cut "frills" such as music, art, physical education, and even kindergarten. David Seeley, president of the Public Education Association in New York City, warns, "Public education is on trial in big cities. If we can't solve the problems, public education won't survive." [3]

Money Matters

Almost everyone agrees that the main trouble is a lack of money. Supplies and maintenance are costing more and more and teachers' unions are demanding more and more. In the 1976-1977 school year there were 152 school districts hit by teachers' strikes, which not only closed the classrooms but also created expensive resolutions.[4]

On the other hand, because many of the big school systems are so scandalously mismanaged even an increase in funding often doesn't help. When Robert Alioto took over as superintendent of the San Francisco Unified School District, he found it in utter chaos. Having spent the majority of the funds on who knows what, school officials had finished the 1972–1973 school year on a pencil-thin budget.

In New York City, Comptroller Harrison Coldin conducted a full-scale "performance audit" of the Board of Education. He found that only 41 percent of New York's $2.9 billion education budget is spent on classroom instruction for the city's 1 million schoolchildren. The rest goes to support a top-heavy administration. One district was paying twelve more principals than it had schools![5]

Education: Problems Created at Home?

Despite such horror stories, says Wilson Riles, the energetic black superintendent of public education for the State of California, it isn't the bureaucrat's fault alone that big-city schools have become so bad. The schools, he suggests, simply can't cope with today's students—largely the children of the urban black and Hispanic poor. "What we have are parents beset with all kinds of difficulties, not able or not knowing how to take care of their youngsters." These youngsters, he observes, have turned out to be the most difficult student body the nation's schools have ever faced. They arrive unprepared to cope with school, they bring the unruly, irreverent manners of the street into the classroom, and they get little or no help at home since their parents are usually poorly educated.[6]

When Education Is Dangerous to Health

Ask almost any teacher what he or she considers the major problem in the changing city classrooms, and the answer will be "discipline." Many teachers feel deserted by the parents, administrators, and legal officials who once supported the teacher's right to keep order. Last year, an eight-year-old boy walked into his third-grade classroom at Public School 27 in Brooklyn, New York, with a loaded .22-caliber pistol. The teacher disarmed the child, marched him down to the principal's office, and recommended he be suspended from school. But no action was taken and the boy was returned to class.[7]

In 1972 the American School Board Journal reported that teaching school is twice as dangerous as working in a steel mill. It estimated that each year 75,000 teachers are injured badly enough to require medical attention. According to the Senate Subcommittee on Juvenile Delinquency, between 1964 and 1968 assaults on teachers increased by 7,100 percent, and unfortunately they are still on the rise in the 1970s![8]

Teachers: Under Fire

With increasing frequency, America's 2.2 million public school teachers are receiving failing grades from the public they serve. All across the nation declining test scores, widespread functional illiteracy among junior high and high school students and sporadic teachers' strikes, along with other developments, have angered and alienated parents and taxpayers. Teachers have found themselves caught in a cross fire. They are pressured by parents and school administrators to promote pupils whether or not they are qualified and then blamed for the pupils' poor performance.[9]

Commenting on this situation, Terry Herndon, executive director of the National Education Association (NEA) said, "Teachers are under more pressure than ever, and they are more frustrated than ever. We live in a turbulent, neurotic society, and that society comes to school every day." Teachers feel too many citizens expect the public schools to be all things to all people, and that they are required to assume the role of baby-sitter and social worker as well as that of instructor.[10]

Until very recently, teachers were highly esteemed but poorly paid. Now, with the advent of unions, teachers are becoming more highly paid, but poorly esteemed. As annual expenditures for public education approach $70 billion, teachers are being held accountable for their teaching—or their lack of teaching. Some parents and students have filed malpractice suits against school systems, claiming they fail to adequately educate and prepare students for the working world.[11]

Valueless Education

Throughout history, the public schools have always represented and transmitted certain basic values, but today the public school in America is trying to fill so many disparate needs it's becoming a neutral institution—representing nothing and having no sense of direction. It's lost some of its moral center. That's why courses such as "Value Clarification" have been added to the curriculum. When education is morally neutral, special classes have to be developed to communicate to students what values are all about.[12]

The obvious and observable outcome of education without values is chaos, both in and out of the classroom and throughout the entire system. As the results of valueless education have become more and more destructive, the demands for values to be returned to education have grown. The problem now is what value system should be taught?

Educating children and young adults in values necessitates some type of involvement by the parents, since parents are the initial and primary models for their children's value systems. A recent Gallup poll reported parental apathy as one of the public's top educational concerns, and teachers responding to a National Education Association survey stated their No. 1 instructional concern was "parental lack of interest." Professionals are now making the unsettling discovery that schools and colleges can't produce either educated or well-adjusted young people without parental and community cooperation in the process of instilling values.[13]

Educationless Education

Valueless education leads to educationless education and for United States educators, that means the start of a new and critical era in which quality is becoming a major concern. Disillusioned with progressive education, the public is pressuring them to return to the basics of reading, writing, and arithmetic.[14]

Critics complain that teachers are no longer educators, but only entertainers and peacemakers. Mary Ellen Smith, a leader of the City-wide Education Coalition, a probusing group, said, "The issue is no longer where kids go to school or the race of their classmates, but whether the public schools can offer a quality education."[15] Dr. Max Rafferty, former California State Superintendent of Public Instruction, says in his book, *Suffer, Little Children*, "There is really only one great problem in American education today; all others stem from it, and will be on the way toward solution when it is solved. This is the tragedy of declining standards."[16]

There has been a major shift in educational theory, placing the emphasis not on rising above, altering and remolding one's environment, but on adjusting to it. This great dogma of Group Adaption now sits as the cornerstone of twentieth-century educational thinking. As laid down by the pragmatic philosophers, who paradoxically profess to abhor all dogma, the only eternal verity is constant change and flux: *All values are relative. All truths are mutable. All standards are variable.* The only thing worth teaching young people is the ability to adjust to this constantly moving environment kaleidoscope. It's a roller coaster philosophy of life, and it's taking us on a joy ride to nowhere. "Young people have been educated to conform, conditioned to cooperate, trained to adjust. In another generation or two they should be ready for the bee hive."[17]

It's educationless education. It's not the "what" any longer, but the "how." Not individualism, but utilitarianism. Not knowledge imparted, but behavior produced. Not altering, but adjusting to the environment. Not acting, but reacting. *Education is no longer education! It's training!*

Training Is Not Education

Training is not education! Typists, mechanics, and plumbers, for example, may be thoroughly trained and highly proficient in particular skills and yet virtually uneducated in the broad liberal sense. Their own narrow specialties may be the only thing they know. That is vocational training—not education.[18]

Commenting on the difference, Edmund Opitz, a staff member of the Foundation for Economic Education, said: "It is needful that men possess such skills as the ability to lay bricks and cut hair. . . . But while the possession of such skills is desirable and important, their exercise is not the distinctive mark of an educated man. It is true, however, that an educated man ought to have a quiverful of such and similar talents. . . . But this is merely to say that a man ought to be trained as well as educated." [19]

"Treatment" Is Not Education

The new object of education is behavioral control through such methods as *operant conditioning*—a system of shaping behavior through positive reinforcement. Although there does seem to be some merit in this "lollipop" method, it also seems it could be taken too far.

In B. F. Skinner's *Walden Two,* one of the main characters reasoned: "When a science of behavior has once been achieved, there's no alternative to a planned society. We can't leave mankind to an accidental or biased control. When you have once grasped the principle of positive reinforcement, you can enjoy a sense of unlimited power. It's enough to satisfy the thirstiest tyrant." [20]

For those who wish to train "social animals," the field of education offers a green and fertile pasture in which to do so. The opportunities there are irresistible and unsurpassed, for not only are the "animals" captive, they are also young and "flexible." There is less to be "unlearned" and "relearned" than would be the case with "rigid" adults. And, when enough of these young ones are properly "shaped" and headed in the "right" direction, virtually the whole herd may be guided like sheep down the primrose path—wherever the "change agent" leadeth them! [21]

The "change agent" or controller of the student's behavior is naturally the teacher. "Forecast for the '70s," published in *Today's Education—NEA Journal*, stated that in ten years it would be more accurate to call teachers "learning clinicians." The article conveyed the idea that schools are becoming "clinics," with the purpose of providing individualized psychosocial "treatment" for the student. "Facilities will include both biochemical therapists and pharmacists." [22]

Will it be "psychosocial" clinics instead of schools? "Clinicians" instead of teachers? "Therapy" or "treatment" instead of education? Will our children be their guinea pigs? [23]

John I. Goodlad, Dean of the UCLA Graduate School of Education, expressed the most crucial issue in the educational time bomb: "The most controversial issues of the twenty-first century will pertain to the ends and means of modifying human behavior and who shall determine them. The first educational questions will not be, 'What knowledge is of most worth?' but 'What kinds of human beings do we wish to produce?' The possibilities virtually defy our imagination." [24] When Hitler tried to breed a "pure race," the world rightly denounced him. Why is the same thing unobjectionable when it's sponsored by the National Education Association?

Instant and Boundless Education

We are headed toward a Brave New World of technological teaching. Increasingly sophisticated audio, video, and computer technologies will soon replace the three R's as the primary tools of communication. The "basics" of reading, writing, and arithmetic have always been considered essential tools, necessary prerequisites for knowledge, communication, and even wisdom. But, by the time today's four-year-old reaches adulthood, there won't be any compelling reason for him to be proficient in the "basics."

He will have more—not less—access to the accumulated wisdom of the world, and the three R's will have succumbed to the influence of fast, inexpensive, and reliable computers that can call up information instantly in response to a few spoken words. Electronic media will make everything there is to know universally accessible to all people. Knowledge will then be everyone's property, rather than being restricted to the minority who can afford the luxury of acquiring it.[25] Every indication suggests that twenty-first century America may be a society in which knowledge, ability, and wisdom are exceedingly widespread in a population that is substantially illiterate.[26]

Eventually we may have the solution to end all solutions: *instant learning*—just a teaching machine next to your pillow at night—and plug in! How much you sleep, not how much you study, would determine how much you learn. A group of University of Wisconsin professors are investigating how to transmit a pattern of electrical charges representing the configuration of a particular body of knowledge to our nervous system. Do you want to learn Italian? They would wrap a band around your wrists, pull a switch, and you walk away saying, "Grazi. Le sono molto grato." When the headlines announce this ultimate breakthrough, colleges can forget rote learning. The only curriculum needed then would be that concerned with the thinking process (if anyone was still interested in such a thing).[27]

In addition to instant learning there is the information explosion occurring through the tools of informal education—TV, radio, newspapers, magazines, and books. The bombardment comes from every angle—it's impossible to escape!

For instance, between 1950 and 1976 the circulation of major magazines jumped from 147.3 million to almost 255 million. Between 1975 and 1976 their advertising pages increased 17 percent. Last year alone, according to *Folio*, 336 new magazines were started. Trivia, gossip, sex, and leisure are currently the "hot" topics for articles in today's magazines —and many of them include material that would have shocked the average sensible reader of a few years ago.[28]

Meanwhile, daily newspapers have experienced a dip in

their weekday circulation between 1973 and 1976. They fell from 63.1 to 60.9 million, though a slight rising trend is now becoming visible.[29]

The primary source of news and information in the U.S. is television. Sixty-four percent of Americans say they get most of their news from TV, and a majority of them find it the most believable medium.[30] In an average day, 92 percent of all TV households are reached by TV and 98 percent are reached in an average week. In 1975, for the twenty-first consecutive year TV was the number one medium for the top 100 national advertisers.[31]

About 73 million households, or 97 percent of American residences, have television sets, and nearly 45 percent of them have more than one. Among its viewers, adult women clock more tube time than any other group, averaging 30 hours and 14 minutes a week. Children from ages 2 to 11 average 25 hours and 38 minutes, adult men 24 hours and 25 minutes, and teenagers 12 through 17 average 22 hours and 36 minutes a week.[32]

The educational time bomb is triggered by education without values, education that is "training" or "treatment" but not learning, and education that is instant and boundless. As the "controls" of the "clinicians" and the overwhelming information explosion make their marks on society, what will society be: a herd of higher animals, a complex computer, or an illiterate genius? More importantly, who is the controller and the clinician and the dispatcher of the fragmented bits of information aimed at our psyches? Whatever became of Dick and Jane?

Little boy blue, come blow your horn,
The sheep's in the meadow, the cow's in the corn;
But where is the boy who looks after the sheep?
He's under the haystack fast asleep.
Will you wake him? No, not I,
For if I do, he'll be sure to cry.

Little Boy Blue

8

'...For Which It Stands'?
The Political Time Bomb

TEDDY ROOSEVELT WAS INTERRUPTED during a campaign speech by a man in the audience who kept yelling out, "I'm a Democrat." Roosevelt stopped his speech and addressed the heckler, "May I ask the gentleman why he is a Democrat?" The man proudly replied, "My grandfather was a Democrat and my father was a Democrat. That's why I am a Democrat!" Roosevelt shook his head and replied, "And suppose your grandfather was a jackass and your father was a jackass. Then what would you be?" "A Republican," answered the heckler.

No matter the political party, each person must face the many volatile issues of the political time bomb. The economy, social welfare, foreign policy, and bureaucracy, are devastating enough taken one at a time. With all of them exploding at the same time, it's deadly!

The Economy: Legalized Counterfeiting

If a private business was caught printing counterfeit money, even if they had a good reason for doing so, they'd be forced to close their doors and compensate their customers for any losses. However, there is one exception to this rule, and it's made for the only guy who could get away with it—

Uncle Sam! Whenever the government needs more money, either to meet interest payments on its escalating debt or keep up with its overembellished budget, it prints more money, and even though these extra dollars are legal in the technical sense, they are counterfeit in that there's nothing to back them up. Distributed as legal tender, they only reduce the value of the dollars already in circulation and invest our economy with the cancerous disease of inflation.

Inflation is not caused by higher prices, higher wages, an increase in the cost of living, or the shrinking value of the dollar. Those are the consequences, the symptoms, or visible signs of inflation. Inflation is caused by an increase in the amount of money—both of currency and credit—being poured into the economy. And it can't be stopped until the "counterfeit" money stops coming in.[1]

The price tags on government operations have gone higher and higher every year, and it's eye opening to examine some of the things they're attached to:

*Social welfare programs—costs of these programs have sky-rocketed from $23.5 billion a year in 1950 to $251 billion in 1973.
*Foreign aid—$170 billion, from 1964 to 1974 (plus an additional $94 billion in interest charges on those borrowed funds).
*Wars—more than $150 billion for the Vietnam War alone.
*Farm programs—$25 billion for "farm price and income stabilization" from 1968 to 1972, distributed primarily to corporate and wealthy farm interests.
*Housing programs—$12 billion in urban renewal from 1949 to 1971 (that $12 billion built 200,687 housing units and destroyed 538,044, for a net loss of 337,357 units).
*Giveaway programs—more than 10,000 of them as listed in the 1,000-page *Encyclopedia of U.S. Government Benefits*, W. H. Wise & Co., 1965.
*General funds—for the swollen costs of extra-curricular activities (that have mushroomed from $20 billion a year in 1940 to almost $500 billion in 1975). Included in those rising costs were such noteworthy projects as . . . $35,000 to chase wild boars in Pakistan, $70,000 to study the smell of sweaty Australian bushmen, $250,000 a year to run the Interdepartmental Screw Thread Committee (established in WW I), $6,000 to study bisexual frogs in Poland, $20,000 to research cockroaches in Germany, $84,000 to study why people fall in love,

$260,000 to investigate the seeds of "passionate love," and $2 million to buy a luxury yacht for Marshal Tito of Yugoslavia.[2]

The U.S. News and World Report disclosed, "Wrathful constituents are bombarding Congressmen with protests against such federal projects as these: $375,000 for a Pentagon study of the frisbee; $159,000 to teach mothers how to play with their babies; $80,000 to develop a zero-gravity toilet; $121,000 to find out why some people say 'ain't'; and $29,324 for a study of the mating calls of the Central American toad."

To spend as it does, the government has to borrow money as well as print it; this heavy borrowing by the U.S. Treasury makes it difficult for the Federal Reserve System to control the money supply, and as the money supply grows faster than the nation's productive capacity inflation spreads even further. Most economists believe that debt will, and must, grow as long as the economy grows, and so far that's been the case. Inflation gets the most blame for the rapid rise now occurring. It takes a larger loan to buy a house, a car, a machine or a factory, but inflation also tends to raise incomes and, hence, the borrowing capacity of consumers and businesses.

Inflation also permits debtors to pay with dollars of depreciating value, and because interest is tax deductible, many people figure it pays to borrow. Under such conditions, Ben Franklin's advice to avoid debt and trust to savings is unlikely to be taken by many.[4]

When the federal government can't get its money from the Federal Reserve, it can always resort to taxation. As one economist put it: "Income tax is the fairest of all taxes—it gives everybody an equal chance at poverty." The total cost of all government today—federal, state and local—is estimated at 43 percent of the nation's total personal income and 35 percent of its gross national product. If inflation doesn't consume America's money, then taxation will![5]

According to a study by the National Taxpayers Union (based on official Treasury Department figures), U.S. taxpayers are now on the hook for at least $7.5 trillion. And that astronomical figure was accumulated by expenditures which have brought little or no benefit to the taxpayer:

- $3 billion stolen annually from health programs—yet the federal government has fewer people investigating the theft than it has manicuring the White House lawn.
- $600,000 in subsidy payments to a single beekeeper in Washington.
- $6.5 billion a year for the Pentagon to buy five times as many routine supplies (not weapons) as are actually used, 80 percent of which are later scrapped in unused condition or sold for pennies on the dollar.
- Billions wasted annually on 900,000 "totally ineligible" welfare recipients.
- $200 million annually to perform useless research and shower favored professors with grants. (There are 23 biographies of Isaac Newton in the Library of Congress, yet the federal government wants to spend $10,000 for another one).
- $85,000 per minute to pay interest on the "national debt," costing a total of $318 billion since World War II.
- $250 billion for foreign aid, including the financing of both sides of 14 wars over the last 20 years.[6]

The National Taxpayers Union is working for enactment of two constitutional amendments. One would prohibit the federal government from taking more than 25 percent of an individual's income. As it stands now, a person spends five months a year working to pay all direct and hidden taxes. That's worse than the serfs in the Dark Ages. They were only required to spend three months working for their masters. The remaining nine months they were free to work for themselves. The other amendment would require the federal government to balance its budget. This proposal has already been approved by the legislatures of 21 states and they have threatened to call a constitutional convention if Congress refuses to pass a Balance the Budget amendment.[7]

Social Welfare—Forced Philanthropy?

Approximately 8 percent of the American population receives public assistance payments of one type or another (not including social security, unemployment compensation, and so on, which are funded in part or wholly by private contributions). In the major metropolitan areas, this figure is more than 10 percent and, in some cities—such as San Francisco, Baltimore, New York and St. Louis—the ratio of those who receive government assistance is 1 out of 7. Since 1950, the number of people on welfare has increased from 6,052,000 to almost 18,000,000 in 1974. The number of recipients has almost tripled in the past 24 years.[8]

In 1960 the federal government employed 72,747 people to carry out its various social welfare programs; by 1974 there were 158,904. In addition to the federal numbers, in the same year there were approximately 1,220,000 state and local social welfare workers who were paid a combined annual salary of more than $1 billion.[9]

The largest single welfare category is Aid to Families with Dependent Children (AFDC). In 1973, 3,155,000 families with 7,813,000 children received tax-paid funds through AFDC. Eighteen percent of those families had been on AFDC for 5 years or more and 35 percent had been receiving public assistance payments for 3 or more years.[10]

Only 12 percent, of those more than 3 million AFDC families, had fathers who were deceased or incapacitated. In 83 percent of the homes, he was simply "absent," meaning in most cases that he had skipped out on the mother and children and left the responsibility for them with the taxpayers.[11]

The Tax Foundation has predicted if the present trends continue, more than 21,200,000 people will be receiving public assistance payments by 1980, increasing total expenditures by at least 45 percent. That would mean the payments would total more than $34 billion, and the total cost of the social welfare (all levels of government) would be in the neighborhood of $312 billion a year! No doubt that's one of the factors which prompted former federal budget director Roy Ash to warn President Ford the day may not be too far away when government takes two-thirds of the gross national product![12]

Job Creation—A Boon or Boondoggle?

Despite nagging doubts about their effectiveness, government projects utilize billions of tax dollars to lower unemployment. Now that Congress has voted the money to pay for President Carter's economic-stimulus package, the way is clear for the largest federal effort to create jobs since the Great

Depression. More than $15.9 billion, some of it already spent, has been earmarked to boost public-employment programs.[13]

As billions of dollars are being poured into jobs programs, some crucial questions are being raised: Are federally financed jobs the best means of fighting the unemployment problems? Which programs create the most new jobs at the least cost? What effects do such programs have on private employment? Do they provide meaningful work or just a dead-end for those hired? Are they fairly administered and relatively free of waste? Is this program a boon or a boondoggle?[14]

Supporters claim the additional funding will generate 300,-000 jobs in the private construction industry and another 300,-000 indirectly, but past experience indicates the total may be substantially less. A similar program in the 1960s produced fewer than half the jobs originally predicted. In any case, public works is proving to be an expensive way to attack unemployment. By some estimates, the cost per job created may top $30,000.[15]

Social Security or Insecurity?

Another side of the social welfare crisis is the ailing Social Security system. The 40-year-old program is pumping out more benefits than it's taking in. The short-run drain on the pension reserve is blamed on two developments. First, unemployment of an unusually widespread and persistent nature is depriving the system of its revenue of payroll taxes. Second, inflation is causing the benefits to increase in order to keep up with living costs.[16]

The gap between the system's income and outgo in the fiscal year starting October 1, 1978, is expected to be nearly 7 billion dollars. If Congress doesn't take action soon, the reserve fund that backs up benefits, now containing more than 40 billion dollars, is expected to vanish by 1981.

There are also some long-range problems in the system. With the birth rates declining, 50 percent in the last 20 years, the population is getting older and older. That means fewer people are reaching working age in relation to those who are drawing old-age benefits. There are now only 31 beneficiaries for every 100 workers, but in another 70 years there will be 50 beneficiaries for each 100 workers. The strong medicine prescribed by President Carter for the ailing Social Security system involves a massive shift of its tax burden from people on the low end of the wage ladder to those on the middle and upper-middle rungs. If Congress goes along with Carter's proposals for curing the system's ills, lower-income people will get substantial relief while those with annual earnings in the range of $16,000 to $35,000, particularly executives and self-employed people, will have to pay the majority of Social Security's taxes.[19]

Overall, Carter's plan for dealing with the failing finances of Social Security would have repercussions for almost everyone in the working world, and as Congress moves to deal with his proposals, they are certain to generate controversy.[20] The Social Security system may be becoming more secure, but at whose expense?

Bureaucracy—Who Done It?

A bureaucrat is someone who sees his duty and then gets someone else to do it! And with 14 million people on Uncle Sam's payroll there must be a lot to do. Not only is the government bureaucracy big business, it's also a well paying business. With employees already averaging more than $15,000 a year, plus fringe benefits, another big pay raise is in the works. With the proposed 7.05 percent increase, the average federal employee would be making approximately $17,350 a year, plus fringe benefits. When this new raise takes effect, Government white-collar workers will have received 12 raises since mid-1967, boosting their pay 94.8 percent.[21]

Some critics of the latest increase have raised the question of whether Uncle Sam, as the nation's largest employer, is going to add to the upward trend in labor costs for other employers and give inflation another boost. When federal pay jumps, it adds pressure for higher pay in many areas, especially in state and local governments. Another question asked by critics (and by citizens) is, are most government employees already overpaid, even before the new raise?[22]

The expensive package of bureaucracy comes lavishly wrapped in red tape! It costs business and industry (and thus the consumer) almost $20 billion a year to handle the paper work involved with government regulations. It costs government (and thus the consumer) another $20 billion a year to pay for its printers and processors and papershufflers. That's $40 billion a year for triplicate forms, filing cabinets, postage stamps, and wastepaper baskets. And most, if not all, of it is counterproductive.[23]

It took 1100 different permits and approvals before the construction of the Alaska pipeline could begin. When the project was first proposed, the estimated cost was $1 billion. After years of political demagoguery and governmental foot-dragging, the estimated costs now stand at more than $6 billion, and politicians and bureaucrats won't foot that increase. The consumer will, through higher prices.[24]

Foreign Policy—Buy Back America?

An area of major concern in U.S. foreign policy is the gross imbalance of trade. Many American businesses are finding it increasingly difficult to compete with foreign companies. Since 1970, the amount of goods imported has grown at a faster pace than those exported. The shift began in the years prior to 1970. During the period between 1965 to 1970, while exports were increasing at a rate of 10 percent a year, imports were increasing at the rate of 14 percent per year. In 1974 imports rose one-third more rapidly than the increase in exports, and in 1974—for the first time since the depressed years of 1935–1940 —imports exceeded exports.

The impact of such a trade deficit may not seem crucial to many Americans, but it does put a drain on our economy. Every dollar in imports means dollars and jobs going to competing industries in competing nations instead of to companies here.[25] We are being sold out to other countries. *Not only is our nation out of control, but we don't even own it!* Maybe the time has come to buy back America!

There are many other critical issues in the political time bomb, such as the arms race, detente, crime (organized and unorganized), energy, and so on. But the political time bomb can best be summed up this way: *people controlled by an uncontrolled government.*

Three men went for a long walk—a doctor, an architect, and a politician—and they began discussing whose profession was the oldest. The doctor said, "My profession is the oldest, since God created Eve out of Adam's rib and performed a surgical operation." The architect replied: "My profession is still older, since God, just like any architect, in creating the world made it out of chaos!" "Ah," joined in the politician, "but who made the chaos?"

Peter, Peter Pumpkin-eater,
Had a wife and couldn't keep her;
He put her in a pumpkin shell,
And there he kept her very well.
                        Peter Peter Pumpkin-eater

9

As the World Turns:
The Sociological Time Bomb

TWO AMERICAN INDIANS WERE talking things over in a fox-hole between air raids during World War II. "The way I figure it," one said, "is that when they smoked the peace pipe in 1918, nobody inhaled!" In our world of sociological sabotage more and more relationships have been breaking up and falling into the witch's cauldron—which is boiling with toils and troubles! Whether between nations, minorities, neighbors, or families, relationships are rampant with conflict and pain. Among nations (the family of man), the twentieth century has given us more wars than all of the previous centuries put together. Among families (man's family), marriages aren't working, parenting is less effective, and individuals are obsessed with self-satisfaction. *The essence of the sociological time bomb is the turmoil of relationships!*

Mass Society

A mass society is not characterized by large numbers, or rather by large numbers alone, but by its concentration and density. Vast land-mass societies have had large populations for a long time, but they were always spread out over an immense area and were primarily segmental rather than integral in their social organization. It's only been since the segmentation has broken down and people have come into increasingly close contact and interaction with each other—in large urban concentrations, or through mass communication—that a mass society has emerged.

Daniel Bell, professor of sociology at Harvard University, calls the mass society an "eclipse of distance." The initial changes caused by a mass society are the result of new forms of transportation and communication which bring people into ready contact with each other. The "eclipse of distance" is not only the foreshortening of time and space in flying across continents or in being in instant communication with any part of the globe by satellite or radio, it is also an eclipse of social, esthetic, and psychic distance as well.[1]

In many ways the United States, with all its historical particularity, has acquired the features of a mass society. Even though some political influences remain, regionalism as a form of cultural segmentation has largely broken down. Family-based enterprises of farms, retail establishments, and small manufacturing businesses have been bought up by large corporations, and those remaining play a minor role in the economy. With the average household moving on the average of once every five years, the mobility of individuals, both spatial and social, is unprecedented in history. The effects of this mobility and the increase in number, interaction, and density of population are enormous.[2]

The mass society suffers from a lack of insulated space and a communication overload. In the past, people in the U.S. were somewhat insulated from news and information. By the time they heard about something it was impossible to do anything about it either because of time (too late to act) or distance (too far to go).

The mass media made possible, and continues to provide for, the spectacular rise in "participatory democracy," but all too often it arises out of an emotional issue. When that happens the loss of insulating space then allows a chain reaction to be set off which may be detrimental to both politics and reasoned debate.[3]

There are enormous problems arising from the communication overload. Because of our current psychological values we are placing a greater emphasis on the individual. Yet, at the same time, there is less possibility of privacy, of obtaining a "psycho-social moratorium" (a term originated to describe the need of sensitive adolescents to escape the pressures of schools, career choice, adult responsibilities, and so on). Is it even possible to find open spaces and relief from the incessant communication, and if so, where? [4]

Mass Society: Colleagues in Crime

According to the tabulations for 1976, crimes against people—murder, forcible rape, aggravated assault and robbery—fell almost 4 percent, while crimes against property—burglary, larceny-theft, and vehicle theft—rose nearly 1 percent. Serious crime in metropolitan areas and small cities was down about 1 percent but rose some 2.5 percent in rural areas. Even though the increase in crime seems to have halted, there still is a greater incidence of crime in the U.S. today than there was five years ago. In 1976, 11,304,770 serious crimes were reported to the FBI, with crimes of violence numbering nearly 1 million and those against property more than 10 million. The crime rate is up 33 percent from 1972 and 76 percent from 1967. With crime at record levels, the experts aren't very encouraged by the apparent slowdown. In fact, some are expecting serious trouble in the near future. [5]

Division Chief Paul Montoya, head of the detective division of the Denver police department, said, "I am concerned with the juvenile area, especially the marked increase in violence. We as a nation have not figured out how to deal with juvenile crime. We don't know how to separate those who are truly criminal from those who can be rehabilitated. Every state is groping with this problem. Even the federal government doesn't know where to go." [6]

Kids: Getting Away with Murder

People have always accused kids of getting away with murder. However, in the past it was only a clever hyperbole for childish behavior. Today it's no longer only a literary exaggeration. Across the U.S., a pattern of crime has emerged that is both appalling and perplexing. Many youngsters appear to be robbing, raping, maiming, and murdering as casually as if they were going to a movie or joining in on a neighborhood baseball game. A new, mutant, remorseless juvenile seems to have been born, and there is no figure more terrifying on America's crime scene today.

More than half of all serious crimes (murder, rape, aggravated assault, robbery, burglary, larceny, and motor vehicle theft) in the U.S. are committed by youths aged ten to seventeen. Since 1960, juvenile crime has risen twice as fast as adult crime. In San Francisco, kids of seventeen and under are arrested for 57 percent of all crimes against people and 66 percent of all crimes against property. Last year in Chicago, one-third of all murders were committed by people aged 20 or younger, a 29 percent jump over 1975. Last year, in Detroit, youths committed so much crime that city officials were forced to impose a 10 p.m. curfew for anyone 16 or under.[7]

Charles King, the black director of the Phoenix School, which provides therapy and schooling for 30 problem kids on Manhattan's upper west side, thinks inconsistent family treatment is more damaging to children than unrelieved harshness. First the parent strikes the child, and then turns around and lavishes gifts on him. The child is bewildered. He has no way of knowing what's wrong, and he remains largely illiterate because no one talks to him. "His language," says King, "is not made to communicate, to establish relationships. It's rejection and rejection, it's the hell with it. The child learns that the only way to be heard is to kick somebody in the teeth. With violence, he suddenly becomes a being." [8]

Unfortunately the media often helps in teaching youngsters to be heard by violence, and the courts encourage their behavior by delivering lenient and excusatory decisions. In Madison, Wisconsin, Dane County Judge Archie Simonson released a 16-year-old rapist into the custody of his family. Madison, the judge explained, is a sexually permissive city where women wear see-through blouses, and though the 16-year-old victim was wearing an unprovocative sweater the boy was only reacting "normally." [9]

But surely these and similar arguments, which go to any length to hold society and not the individual accountable, are glib and shallow. The juvenile justice system, a sieve through which most youth offenders pass without receiving either punishment or rehabilitation, has become a big part of the problem. The court does not consider a child a criminal—irresponsible, perhaps, but not a criminal. It carries out the child's belief that he can beat the system. He goes through the court, comes back to the neighborhood, and he's a hero. [10]

Not the Upper, nor the Middle, but the Underclass

This is a term which is shocking to striving, mobile America: the underclass are America's unreachable! Long used in class-ridden Europe, and then applied to the U.S. in the 1960s by Swedish Economist Gunnar Myrdal, it has become a rather common description of those people who are removed from the American dream, those who seem to be more or less permanently stuck at the bottom. Though the underclass includes all races, living in many different places, it is composed primarily of impoverished urban blacks who are still suffering from a heritage of slavery and discrimination. Their world is often a junk heap of rotting housing, broken furniture, crummy food, alcohol, and drugs.

Their bleak environment nurtures values which are usually radically opposed by the majority—even the majority of the poor. As a result, a highly disproportionate number of the nation's juvenile delinquents, school dropouts, drug addicts, and welfare mothers, as well as much of the adult crime, family disruption, urban decay, and demand for social expenditures come from this underclass minority. Monsignor Geno Baroni, an assistant secretary of Housing and Urban Development says, "The underclass presents our most dangerous crisis, more dangerous than the Depression of 1929, and more complex." [11]

Rampaging members of the underclass carried out much of the looting and burning that swept New York's ghettos during the July, 1977, blackout (55 percent of those arrested were unemployed and 64 percent had been booked previously for other offenses), and they are presently responsible for most of the nation's spreading epidemic of youth crime. Certainly, most members of this subculture are not looters or arsonists or violent criminals, but they are so totally detached from the system that many who would not steal or burn or mug themselves will stand by while others do so, sometimes even cheering them on. The underclass, says Vernon Jordan, executive director of the National Urban League, "in a crisis feels no compulsion to abide by the rules of the game because they find that the normal rules do not apply to them." [12]

Underclass Americans number between 7 and 8 million, perhaps even as high as 10 million. Subjected to family structures, competing street values, and lack of hope amidst an affluent society, the American underclass is unique among the world's poor peoples. [13]

Nothing has ever been able to replace individual incentive in U.S. society, and probably never will. The underclass must lend a helping hand in lifting itself out of its morass. More than a century ago Nathaniel Hawthorne observed: "In this republican country, amid the fluctuating waves of social life, somebody is always at the drowning point." Ever since then, though, successive generations of aspiring Americans have lifted themselves above the level of despair. One hopes the desperation, hostility, violence, and disaffection within the underclass is something even the world's wealthiest country can't afford. [14]

Youth gangs aren't "back." They never went away—except in the media. What's new is their wars are growing deadlier, and their enemy is anyone!

In most cities, today's youth gangs typically consist of small, loosely organized groups of about a dozen teenage males. Instead of confining their claims of control to local streets and parks, many gangs have taken over neighborhood

schools and recreational facilities. Along with turf and pres-
tige, their main concern is money. To get it, they shake down
local merchants and make armed, guerrilla-style forays to
carry out muggings, robberies, and burglaries. Instead of
Sharks and Jets (as in West Side Story), they bear names like
Savage Skulls and Black Assassins. Instead of switchblades
and homemade zip guns, they use modern handguns and
sawed-off shotguns. Instead of simply mugging or beating
victims, they may kill or seriously wound them. Instead of
attacking only rival gang members, they increasingly vic-
timize ordinary citizens.[15]

Once the quietest of ethnic neighborhoods, Chinatown is
now exploding with violence. A 10-year flood of young immigrants, coming mainly from Hong Kong, has brought a wave
of crime and fear. Until the quotas were lifted in 1965, the
Chinese population in New York City remained around 10,-
000. Since then, the city's Chinese population has increased
to more than 150,000, with 30,000 to 50,000 of them crammed
into Chinatown. About 20,000 more Chinese are entering the
U.S. every year, and nearly half of them settle in New York.
It's been from this expanding immigrant population that the
youth gangs have formed, but they're not just youth gangs.
They are mean, and they mean business.[16]

In recent years all types of gangs have been making more
assaults on ordinary citizens. Figures for cities in which information is available show a fairly consistent pattern: 60 percent of the victims of gang violence are gang members, the
rest are outsiders. In New York and Los Angeles, for example,
gang members have been committing an increasing number of
crimes in middle-class residential and commercial areas.[17]
There have also been numerous reports of gang attacks on
women, children, and particularly, the elderly.

Organized Crime: It's All in the Family

As during Prohibition, big-time criminals profit by providing goods and services that are either illicit or in scarce
supply and hard to acquire. The Mafia now dominates the
production and distribution of pornographic books, maga-

zines, and movies, a business that has doubled in the last decade to $2.2 billion a year. It has also become heavily involved
in bootleg cigarettes and coffee. Most of the mob's mainstay
businesses are profiting more than ever: gambling, narcotics,
loan-sharking, extortion, hijacking and labor racketeering.[18]

No one outside the tight-knit Mafia organization knows the
full extent of its operations, but figures gathered from a variety of law enforcement agencies estimate the Mafia takes in at
least $48 billion in annual gross revenues and nets an in-
credible $25 billion or more in untaxed profits. By contrast,
Exxon, the largest industrial corporation in the U.S., reported
sales of $51.6 billion and net profits of $2.6 billion in 1976.[19]

Considering the impact it has on American life, the Mafia
is a remarkably small organization. According to the FBI, the
Mafia only numbers about 5,000 "made men," or members.
All are of Italian ancestry and most have their roots in Sicily.
Of course, the number of mobsters involved in organized
crime nationwide is far higher and has no ethnic limits. "Red-
necks" dominate the Georgia underworld. Blacks and His-
panics run most of the neighborhood rackets. Jews, Greeks,
Chinese, and Irish Americans all have their own particular
areas.

Dominating much of American crime, the Mafia is by far the
most highly organized criminal group in the U.S. and the
only one with a national structure: 26 families, 5 of them in
New York City, including from 20 to 1,000 "button men," or
soldiers. Many nonmember gangsters are allied to it, usually
kicking back a share of their take to the dons (the "bosses"),
and some criminologists estimate that these confederates of
the Mafia number at least 50,000.[20]

Increasing amounts of mob money are being poured into
real estate, construction companies, trucking firms, meat-
packing, vending machines, liquor stores, laundries, hotels,
restaurants, and bars. In fact, no facet of U.S. commercial life
is safe from Mafia infiltration in the form of investment offers.
The Mafia may own as many as 10,000 legitimate firms, which
generate profits estimated at $12 billion.[21]

The criminal violence from organized and disorganized

groups alike has both sickened and eroded the mass society. Yet an equal and even more subtle contributor to the erosion has come from the "normal" segment of society.

The Leisure Boom: Wall-to-Wall Playpen!

Never in history have leisure and recreation attained the status they now enjoy in the U.S. As measured by the money people have spent on them, leisure-time activities have risen almost unnoticed to become the nation's No. 1 industry. Figures compiled by the Economic Unit of *U.S. News & World Report* show that Americans spent approximately $160 billion on leisure and recreation in 1977. By 1985, the total is expected to climb to $300 billion. Leisure and its various by-products have become so important in America's daily life that more than 300 universities and colleges offer "leisure studies," which in some cases lead to careers in park and recreation management.[22]

A wide spectrum of pleasures—whether wild or wearying—is keeping today's young adults on the go. They jog, learn karate, dangle from hang gliders, and raise snakes as pets. They meet in spas to have their bodies splashed with cold water and slapped with palm fronds. Some go to discos, some to orgies, and some to tea dances.[23]

Although leisure and recreational activities are extremely effective in counteracting the stresses of our society, their effect upon the workplace may not be so positive. Along with family life, work and leisure are always competing for people's time and attention. One or the other usually wins out, and rarely is an individual able to strike an equal balance between all three. For the New Breed, family and work have grown less important while leisure has grown more important. When work and leisure are compared as sources of satisfaction, only one out of five people states that work is more fulfilling to him than leisure. The preoccupation with self, which is the hallmark of New Breed values, has placed the burden of providing work incentives more squarely on the employer, as opposed to the employee under the old value system. The problem this creates in the workplace is, how do you motivate people toward greater productivity when they find little or no satisfying identity in their work? [24]

Rebels Are Now Adults

The minority of those who were in the forefront of the 1960s youth rebellion went on to adopt a very conventional life style, but the activities of their generation as a whole still remain considerably different from their parents in such matters as sex, family life, attitudes toward work, politics, and so on. Now as young adults, they have undermined the basic unit of society—the nuclear family. For one thing, people of this generation are not raising as many children, and many have chosen to remain childless. For another, the greater incidence of divorce means that a large percentage of the children they do have become the product of what used to be called broken homes. Now they are called single-parent households, in keeping with the changing concepts of family life.[25] Furthermore, this change has been brought about by various other upheavals which are strongly supported by this generation, such as the women's lib movement and the larger number of working women.[26]

In an interview with James S. Coleman, Professor of Sociology at the University of Chicago, he commented: "I think we are becoming the first species in the history of the world which is unable to care for its young. Over all, child rearing is one of the biggest casualties of the modern age that is being ushered in by this generation."[27]

When asked what accounts for this declining interest in children, Dr. Coleman said: "It's because the value system that used to hold families together has been turned upside down. Now the husband and wife typically put their own individual interests first, their joint goals second, and any family interests beyond the couple third. That is a reverse order from the traditional ranking that placed family concerns first and individual goals last. Because the fundamental reversal of priorities leads to more divorce and parental neglect, it has serious implications for stability of the family. Of all the changes these young adults are bringing into society, I think this breakdown of the family is going to prove to be the most powerful, the most destructive and the most enduring."[28]

Individual: Swallowed Up by the Mass Society

In the past, the only demand made on society was to support the individual, to allow him to be himself. But, the individual today doesn't know who he is, he's looking to society not only for support, but for identity as well. As he looks out over our sick and ever-changing society for a reflection of who he is, he's overwhelmed with feelings of anonymity and loneliness—a real orphan of the universe! That's the sociological time bomb, and there are as many variables as there are people. *The cauldron of mass society continues to boil with the toils and troubles of relationships!*

Three wise men of Gotham
Went to sea in a bowl:
If the bowl had been stronger,
My song would have been longer.
Three Wise Men of Gotham

10

How to Handle a World:
The Philosophical Time Bomb

IF YOU BUILD CASTLES in the air, your work need not be lost; that is where they should be. Now put foundations under them." *Henry David Thoreau.* The preceding time bombs place your feet firmly in midair. The philosophical time bomb keeps them there, by pulling the rug or foundation out from under you!

Who Pulled That Rug?

Daniel J. Boorstin, director of the National Museum of Science and Technology at the Smithsonian Institution, describes our current situation this way: ". . . we have lost our sense of history . . . lost our traditional respect for the wisdom of ancestors and the culture of kindred nations. Flooded by screaming headlines and hourly televised 'news' melodramas of dissent and 'revolution,' we haunt ourselves with the illusory ideal of some 'whole nation' which had a deep and outspoken 'faith' in its 'values.'"[1]

Arthur M. Schlesinger, Jr., Albert Schweitzer Professor of Humanities at the City University of New York, declared: "Improved methods of medical care and nutrition have pro-

duced the population crisis; and the growth and redistribution
of population have produced the urban crisis. The feverish
increase in the gross national product first consumes precious
natural resources and then discharges filth and poison into
water and air; hence the ecological crisis. Nor can one omit
the extraordinary moral conditions of poverty, discrimination,
and oppression that mankind has endured for centuries."[2]

The politicians keep assuring us everything is going to work
out, and technology crises may occur now and then, but we're
always told they can be handled. We live in an ingenious age
—in a miracle world where anything can happen. At first we
were fascinated, spellbound, and excited about its endless
possibilities, but we are no longer amazed and not the least
bit amused. Neither are we comforted or reassured. A world
where anything can happen is super, but one in which anything and everything does actually happen is scary!

Now what? How can we still the restless waves and turn
the tide? How can we correct what is basically wrong, and
just what is basically wrong in the first place? Have people
totally shed their sense of morality? Have the rules of expe-
diency, success, and technological triumph replaced the necessity for moral integrity? Everything was "succeeding" for a
while, and progress was the order of the day. Now the new
gods seem to have failed us, and the old God is said to be
dead. Things aren't looking too good—everything's going
wrong!

Who's to blame for all this? Who sickened our air and
oceans? Who blackened our rivers and lakes? Who beggared
our paupers? Who crushed our blacks? Who alienated our
youth? Who started the wretched, interminable war? Who
corrupted our business morals, our politics, our judicial system? No one? Who caused all these calamities? Is no one to
blame when so much has gone wrong, or could it be that man
himself is to blame?[3]

Man has pulled the rug out from under himself, and now
he has nothing to stand on. He's created a cultural crisis, and
neither the politicians nor the technicians can resolve it for

him. Its roots lie deep in the values which sustain or fail to support a system. Daniel Bell, author of *The Coming of Post-Industrial Society*, says, "The lack of a rooted moral belief system is the cultural contradiction of the society, the deepest challenge to its survival."[4]

Permissiveness: Doing Your Own Thing!

In his book entitled *Christian Freedom in a Permissive Society*, the former Bishop of Woolwich, John Robinson, defined "permissiveness," as "freedom from interference or control, doing your own thing, love, laxity, licence, promiscuity—and, in terms of verbs, swinging, sliding, eroding, condoning, not only by the sanctions of the criminal law, but by any authority whatsoever—parental, professional, civil or even the social constraints, which are imposed by public opinion. In other words, permissiveness claims that individuals not only have the responsibility to make their own moral decisions, but the right to make them without interference from anyone. If they accept the implications of what they are doing, then it's morally justified."[5]

The Rug Wasn't Pulled—It Disintegrated!

Every ethical belief and moral standard within our culture is in a constant state of disintegration. No matter what the belief or what the standard, they all pass through three very definite steps of disintegration. The first one is: *"It all depends on how you look at it!"* Then, after thinking it over a little bit, the second step comes: *"It really doesn't make any difference how you look at it!"* Finally, the realization of the third step hits: *"I don't think anybody knows how to look at it!"* Disintegration! All that is left is an agnostic approach to ethics and morals. This is exactly the problem we face in the time bombs. No one seems to know "how to look at it."

The Ticking Symphony

The interdependency of all the time bombs is crucial in understanding the philosophical time bomb. There are three major levels dealt with in the time bombs. The first level includes eight time bombs—*three physical* (ecological-chemical-biological), *three metaphysical* (psychological-religious-parapsychological), and *two regulators* (educational-political). The physical and metaphysical time bombs are mind-boggling, frightening, and out of control. Although the regulators are designed to control communications, and communicate controls, both the educational and the political time bombs have a communications overload and are out of control. The collective effect of the first level of time bombs is *the future is out of control.*

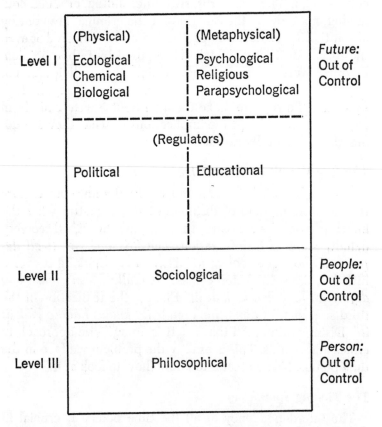

The second level includes only the sociological time bomb,

and the first level rests on it entirely. It's impossible to control the future unless the turmoil of man's relationships is defused, and *people are out of control.*

The third level contains the philosophical time bomb, and it's the foundation for all the others. When a *person and his values are out of control,* relationships don't work and the future doesn't matter.

Do society and science concern themselves with the ethical, social, and human consequences of their acts and achievements? How do we involve them in objectives which will allow people to live a decent, well-rounded life? Who makes the decisions? For example, with genetic engineering, who decides who participates and who the beneficiaries are? Is it made available to everyone, everywhere, or do we just use it for selective breeding?

The essential difference between science and ethics is that science is descriptive while ethics is prescriptive. Science deals with what is, in the indicative mood; ethics deals with what ought to be, in the imperative mood. The validity of scientific theories and statements depends upon verification (are they correct?); that of ethical theories and statements depends upon justification (are they conducive to good?). Science deals with the possible and probable; ethics deals with the preferable. Science will push ahead with what *can* be done; ethics will push ahead for what *should* be done.[7]

When what "can be done" is done with little or no thought as to what "should be done," man becomes alienated from both the biotic and human community. As the ecosystem breaks down it reaches out and breaks up the very heart of our culture. The polluted air and waters are also external signs of ourselves, and in rescuing them we will be rescuing ourselves. The new balance we establish between science and ethics must restore to the individual his heritage of responsibility for the biotic and human community and the treasured insight into his oneness with all of life.[8]

To prevent the breakdown of both our ecosystem and our social system we must be in control, and to be in control, we must have a choice. When there is no choice our actions are only amoral compulsions, and we have lost a distinctive element of our creaturehood.[9]

The bottom line of the three levels of time bombs heard in the ticking symphony always comes to rest on the question of humanness or personness, a concept that is all too rapidly becoming extinct. It's urgent that scientists, philosophers, lawyers, sociologists, and theologians begin to define it. What makes a creature human? A minimum of cerebrocortial function? Self-awareness and self-control? Memory? A sense of time, of futurity? A capacity for interpersonal relationship? Communication? Love? A minimum IQ? Could we add a desire to live? What else? And in what order of priority should we rank them?[10]

Decision Making Is Up for Grabs!

Granted that choices need to be made between "cans" and "shoulds," and about what determines or distinguishes humanness, who is going to make the ultimate decisions? There are really only three alternatives, and all of them are pretty frightening! One possibility is *hedonism,* in which every man does his own thing. However, it quickly destroys any trace of an orderly, civil society because it always leads to chaos. A second possibility is the *51 percent vote.* On this basis, law and morals become a matter of majority; for example, if 51 percent supported it, killing the old, the incurably ill, the insane, or any other group the majority declared to be nonpersons, would be "lawful" and "right."[11]

The third possibility for decision making is an *elite* group of people who would choose the "right and wrong" for everyone else. The Berkeley economist, John Kenneth Galbraith, offered a form of the elite. He suggested it be composed of intellectuals (especially from the academic and scientific world) plus the government. Social economist Robert Theobald has said, "It's naive to deny the necessity for some kind of competent elite."[12] With the intense chaos that has resulted from the time bombs, the possibility of an elite taking control of society is becoming very real. But who or what will control the controllers?

The philosophical time bomb is the most strategic because it affects each of the others, and each of the others has also affected the philosophical. In a sense, man has destroyed (through the time bombs) the base (the issue of the philosophical time bomb) which gives him the possibility of freedom without chaos. Now, not only are man's future and relationships out of control, but man is also out of control. It looks as though man has become *lost* in his own world!

Motorist to native: "Where is the main highway to Quincy?"

Farmer: "I don't know."

Motorist: "Well, where is the highway to Hannibal?"

Farmer: "I don't know."

Motorist: "Where does this highway go?"

Farmer: "I don't know."

Motorist: "You don't know much, do you?"

Farmer: "No, but I ain't *lost*."

Part Two

The Debris
from the Time Bombs

When you repress or suppress those things which you don't want to live with, you don't really solve the problem, because you don't bury the problem dead—you bury it alive. It remains alive and active in you!

John Powell

Not in the clamor of the crowded street,
Not in the shouts and plaudits of the throng,
But in ourselves, are triumph and defeat.

Longfellow

Rain, rain, go away,
Come again another day.
Rain, Rain

11

Shock Waves and Shrapnel

THERE ARE TWO EXTREME approaches to handling life and its debris. One extreme says *life is always being on top of the pile*—filled with optimism—positive with rarely a thought of the negative. When asked, "How are you?", people in this extreme will say, "Super! Fantastic! Couldn't be better!" (Yet even though they have a big smile on the outside, they may be dying on the inside.) In this extreme you have to be on top all the time—exciting everyone about life!

The other extreme says life is always being underneath the pile—filled with pessimism—always dwelling on the negative, with rarely a thought of the positive! "Life is getting worse," warn those in this extreme, "and it probably won't get any better. You'd better come with us to the next life. It will be better there—at least we hope so!" People in this extreme have faces long enough to eat popcorn out of a milk bottle! Instead of *exciting* people about life (as do those who are on top of the pile), they're *embalming* people—preparing everyone for death!

Both of these extremes are wrong! Life is not always being on top and neither is it always being underneath. The position in which you find yourself with life's onslaught will con-

139

stantly differ. You may be on top of a pile or underneath. You may be trying to go around or attempting to shovel through! But no matter where you are or what you're doing, you can't avoid the debris. *Life is full of it!*

If life's struggles only consisted of climbing over, digging under, going around, and shoveling through its piles, then they wouldn't be so difficult to handle. But along with the debris come the psychological and physical struggles of *stress*—the number one health problem in the last decade!

The Stress Mess

Western thinkers divide man into body, mind, and spirit. Physicians treat the body, psychologists and psychiatrists deal with the mind, and the clergy attend to the spirit. In the past, the three areas were most often dealt with separately, but now that we have entered the age of stress, we must deal with the whole person simultaneously. One standard medical text estimates that 50 to 80 percent of all diseases have their origins in stress. Stress-induced disorders have long since replaced infectious disease as the most common maladies of people in the postindustrial nations.[1]

During recent years, heart disorders, cancer, arthritis, and respiratory diseases have become so prominent in the clinics of the United States, Western Europe, and Japan, that they are known as "the afflictions of civilization." Their prevalence stems from poor diet, pollution, and most important, the increased stress of modern society.[2]

The wear and tear of stress is part of the cost of living—no one can avoid it. But for most of us the price has risen too high to pay as we're exposed to the explosion of the time bombs. Modern man faces more daily pressures, such as the unrelenting demands of time, than any other people has at any other time in history. The effect is devastating.

Some people are only vaguely aware of the toll stress is taking on them. Others are acutely aware of it and they have the medical bills to prove it! Things such as financial difficulties, legal entanglements, a business setback, or a death in the family are obvious sources of stress. However, not all stress arises from negative events. Positive occurrences, such as a marriage, a desired pregnancy, a promotion, an outstanding achievement, or even a simple vacation can produce stress. Both winning a lottery and getting a ticket for speeding can make your heart pound, your stomach churn, and your palms sweat. Our bodies exert themselves in much the same way to cope with both desired situations and dreaded events.[3]

The Body's M.O. during Stress

The body's modus operandi or manner of operation (M.O.) for defending itself against stressful situations is extremely complex. Whenever a desired or dreaded stress occurs, the mind rapidly classifies it and sets off the alarm system. The nervous system takes over immediately and makes the necessary adjustments. The pulse rate soars and respiration is retarded. As the blood pressure rises, the heart works harder to distribute the excess supply of blood to the muscles and lungs. All processes in the alimentary canal cease; and the spleen contracts, sending its concentrated corpuscles to predesignated areas. Adrenaline is excreted from the adrenal medulla; sugar is freed from the reserves in the liver; and literally thousands of other complex procedures occur instantaneously and automatically without the individual having to give them the slightest thought. This marvelous transformation, this M.O., protects and provides for the individual in stress.[4]

There's a Tiger Outside

Modern man seldom faces a saber-toothed tiger as his ancestors did. Rather, his defenses are more likely to be required for a chewing out by the boss or a score of less important situations which keep the body constantly on the alert. Thus he is an organism prepared for fight, flight, or freeze, even when nothing is happening or is going to happen. He sits stewing in his own juice—literally—consisting of excess adrenaline and other glandular secretions. The stage is set for anything from a headache to a heart attack.[5]

Many people are so sensitively attuned that it doesn't require a stress of any magnitude to set off their alarm system. It may be a thought, a person's look, a TV program, or simply a plane flying overhead. *The body's chemistry is so severely altered after its defenses are alerted that if no physical action is taken in time various physical or emotional symptoms may occur.* It's like holding the accelerator of a car to the floor while keeping its gears in neutral or its brake on. Going nowhere, the body roars and races, using up energy and wearing out its parts.[6]

Some people's attitudes toward relaxation are very naive. They assume they're relaxed when there is no obvious source of tension. But a person can still have both the mental anxiety and the physical symptoms of prolonged, unabated stress without any identifiable discomfort. For these people, stress is so unremitting they do not even recognize it any more, and this lack of sensitivity can be very dangerous in the long run.[7]

Stress in the Underground

I'm convinced that most of the stress people experience isn't obvious, but having initially gone underground, it sneaks up later without warning to destroy. Sometimes this kind of stress only indirectly affects you and your life, but some time it may directly affect you and end your life.

A few weeks ago I realized I was unusually tense and nervous. My head hurt, my stomach was in knots, and I was beginning to feel depressed. Finally, I retreated to my thinking spot (a local coffee shop) and listed every possible stress I had experienced or been exposed to over the previous two weeks. Here's part of the list I made:

*A close friend called and asked my advice on how to comfort his dad, who was in the hospital, with the news that he was dying of cancer!

*Another close friend shared with me that he felt trapped in his marital, family, and vocational responsibilities and was considering walking out on all of them.

*An extremely successful executive announced that he was going to kill himself and two others.

*Another man threatened to shoot his wife, who had just recently left him.

*A single parent, who had been recuperating from an automobile accident, fell down the stairs. This meant even more time away from her needed employment.

*I finished reading *The Crash of '79*. It seems too possible!

*Another religious cult is in the news accused of "psychological kidnapping." I can't help but think of my own children.

*A woman called from out of state with a tear-jerking story about her daughter's marriage. The husband was frequently beating the daughter (his wife), and he wouldn't allow the parents to see her.

*A prominent couple in our community split up.

*After months of fighting what seems to be a losing battle with an unusual arthritic condition, my colleague was hit with anemia, and his knee swelled up like a grapefruit.

*The first test-tube baby was born. What's next?

*A distant relative in his twenties hanged himself in the bathroom. His wife had also experienced the death of their six-month-old baby the previous year.

*I witnessed a traffic accident in which an eight-year-old boy was mowed down by a truck, which ran a red light.

*I missed my plane because of a traffic jam on the crowded freeway. I was able to make another flight just two minutes before the doors on the plane were shut.

After I had completed my list I realized what had happened. I had allowed myself to become a victim of negative stress! The piles of debris from the shock waves and shrapnel of the various time bombs cannot be escaped, but their damaging effects can be averted! The controlling factor in determining which effect stressful debris will have—healer or slayer—is in the use of the mind!

There are many cases of fatally ill people who have had an unanticipated recovery when they deeply desired to live, perhaps to experience a special event, such as the birth of a grandchild. In other cases fatally ill patients have hung on beyond all expectations, dying only after a significant event, such as the death of a spouse or a birthday. Whatever else may contribute to such miraculous occurrences or timely deaths, it's certain that a person's will to recover or remain alive has a decisive effect on what actually does happen. We have barely begun to comprehend the capacity of a person's mind as healer or slayer.[8]

King Solomon's words concerning the focal point of the mind seem to be more true today than ever before: "*As a person thinks in his heart, so is he!*" How are you thinking?

Today even the survival of humanity is a uto-
pian hope.
Norman O. Brown
You are the orphans in an age of no tomorrows.
Joan Baez
Nature has let us down, God seems to have left
the receiver off the hook, and time is running
out.
Arthur Koestler
Truth stands the test of time: Lies are soon ex-
posed.
King Solomon

12

Cycle of Disintegration

PAUL GOODMAN, A SOCIAL CRITIC in the 1950s, says in his
book, *Growing Up Absurd,* that society is a "closed room in
which there is a large rat race as the dominant center of attention. In the closed room, however, there is only one system of
values, that of the rat race itself. This is shared by everybody
in the room and held in contempt by everybody in the room."[1]

The stress mess brought on by the shock waves and shrapnel of the time bombs will inevitably trigger a cycle of disintegration. The object of this disintegration cycle is mental
health—personness! There are three levels of disintegration,
and each corresponds to one of the three levels of the time
bombs. The first level, *paralysis of fear,* corresponds to the
physical, metaphysical, and regulator time bombs. The second level, *paralysis of anger,* corresponds to the sociological
time bomb. The third level, *paralysis of guilt,* corresponds to
the philosophical time bomb.

These three paralyses of fear, anger, and guilt form a deadly
triad of disintegration. In a sense, fear, anger, and guilt cate-
gorize the stress mess which is out to destroy us, and if you
become caught up in this deadly triad, you are headed toward
something much worse than going over, under, around, or

145

through piles. Instead of maneuvering past the piles of life, you may become one!

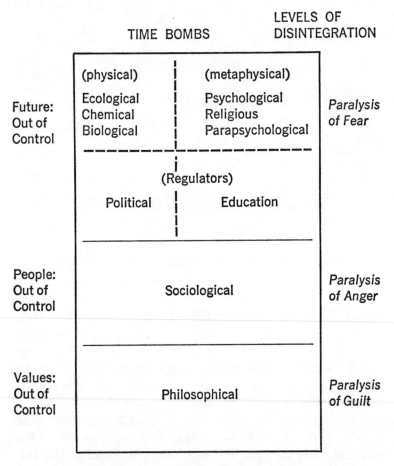

PARALYSIS OF FEAR—HOPELESSNESS

Future: Out of Control

When you are confronted with the tangled web of seemingly insurmountable problems from the time bombs, fear sets in. It's fear of the unknown, a fear of what lies ahead in the future! It's frightening not to know how all the problems will be resolved, and to wonder whether they'll be resolved at all brings on a feeling of hopelessness. As the physical (ecological-chemical-biological), metaphysical (psychological-religious-political) time bombs continue to explode into towering clouds of smoke, the only thing remaining clear is that the future is out of control!

The paralysis of fear includes a sense of inadequacy which may eventually immobilize a person physically as well as psychologically. The loss of this feeling of adequacy is one of the most insidious effects of excessive stress. When an individual is afflicted with physical ailments from unrelenting stress, he frequently feels frustrated, as though he (or any one else for that matter) is unable to help himself.

When stress finally weakens his psychological resistance and his body's immunological response, he may unconsciously link his physical disorder with his psychological and emotional state. This bleak and backward attitude then locks him into an unquestioning acceptance of worsening psychosomatic disorders.[2]

Disease of Destination Sickness

Where am I going? The powerful whirlwind caused by the exploding time bombs is enough to knock you off your feet, and depending on how far you fell and how hard the wind continues to blow, you may not be able to get back on your feet! It's Humpty Dumpty all over again! Add to your bruised bottom and chapped cheeks the nausea and dizziness brought on by the whirling wind, and it becomes virtually impossible to chart a meaningful course for your life. Lying on your back, the best you can do is to shoot randomly out into the future without a target and then draw the target later! This is the disease of destination sickness.

Because the paralysis of fear stems from the out-of-control future, the only "secure" things and actions available are the instant! Our society has been impregnated with instant everything: foods, printing, pictures, films, replays, diets, sex appeal, auto tune-ups, coffee, tea, and so on, ad infinitum. Following on the heels of the instants are the throwaways—diapers, bottles, cans, plates, cups, shavers, clothes, etc., etc., etc.! It's the "now" and the "new"!

The instant and throwaway things in our society do not pose a serious problem by themselves. But the instant and throwaway ways of thinking affect decisions and relationships and therefore create a critical problem. Strategic decisions are made on an "easy" short-term basis with a difficult long-term payoff! Relationships are formed instantly but also tend to be short-term versus long-term! They also get tossed: throwaway relationships and throwaway people!

Lack of Responsibility

The instant and throwaway society breeds a *lack of responsibility!* When something goes wrong, there is a quick move to blame circumstances, objects, or people. Blame something or someone, but whatever you do don't take the blame yourself!

There's a public service announcement on TV that says, "Don't make a good boy go bad"—take your keys and lock your car. As you watch the poor kid steal some negligent guy's car, it's natural to think to yourself, "I certainly don't want to make a good boy go bad!" So there you sit, along with thousands of other people, starting to take the blame for making a good boy go bad. The fact of the matter is that the good boy who climbs in and steals your car goes bad all by himself! You might have made it more convenient for him by leaving your keys in the car, but you are not responsible for the fine young man going bad!

There's quite a market for some bright entrepreneur to be a "professional blamer." He would be hired by the "blamer" to find the best "blamee." A boy shoots his mother and blames Kojak. A student is rejected by a university and sues his high school. A child is disciplined by his parents and files for damages. The next thing may be a person suing his parents for bad hereditary characteristics!

PARALYSIS OF ANGER—LOVELESSNESS

People: Out of Control

The paralysis of fear is primarily concerned about the future, whereas the paralysis of anger is primarily concerned about people. Anger is an attempt to control people or circumstances when they are out of control, and it is, without a doubt, our primary destructive feeling.

Produced in abundance from the sociological time bomb, anger finds many forms of expression. The more overt type of anger is seen in the form of hostility, rage, temper tantrums, sadism, murder, and so on. But there are also concealed forms of anger: suspicion, bereavement, teasing, certain kinds of humor, and depression, which is suppressed anger. The most common and perhaps the most malignant form of anger is resentment. When it's allowed to fester, resentment eventually hardens into an all-consuming bitterness.

Repressed anger can easily take its toll on your body. It may give you a vicious headache, or affect your gastrointestinal system—that thirty-foot tube extending from the "entry" to the "exit"—somewhere along the line. You may experience difficulty in swallowing, nausea and vomiting, gastric ulcer, constipation, or diarrhea. The most common cause of ulcerative colitis is repressed anger, and it's a primary contributor to coronary thrombosis.[4] Respiratory disorders such as asthma are common effects.

A newspaper article reported: "A Southland psychiatrist says that anger and unhappiness are responsible for most heart attacks. Dr. Wallace C. Ellerbroek of Sunset Beach says that learned control of such thoughts is much more important in prevention of heart disease than is strict adherence to a low-cholesterol diet.

"Dr. Ellerbroek, a program director at Metropolitan State Hospital at Norwalk, California, said in an exclusive interview that 'miserable people have a high cholesterol but happy people do not.' 'If you check coronary victims,' he contends, 'you'll find they were either depressed or angry before their coronary.'

"Cholesterol does play a role in heart disease, Dr. Ellerbroek explains, but it is bad emotions, not diet, that send cholesterol levels soaring. For example, he likes to cite a story of Navy flight cadets. On the mornings the cadets were scheduled to fly, their cholesterol ranged from 400 to 650—extremely high. But the mornings they didn't have to fly, their cholesterol levels were 140 to 165, he says—in other words, entirely normal.

"Any negative emotion—anger, depression, frustration, irritation, unhappiness, the blues—is going to affect the entire body and brain adversely to some degree, he maintains."[5]

Disease of Apathy

Rather than endure the pain of verbally expressing angry feelings as they occur, most people choose the repression route. They become pros at throwing their angry thought down into the subconscious and by doing so they develop a pressure-cooker life style—boiling with resentment and periodically blowing up! Fearful of what might be discovered if their cover was ever blown, and harboring anger from previous encounters with intimacy, increasing numbers of people are catching the disease of apathy.

Apathy is characterized by two impoverished values: personal peace and affluence. Personal peace means to be let alone, not to be bothered by other people's troubles, whether the other people are across the world or across the city or next door—to line one's life with minimal possibilities of being personally disturbed. It means wanting to have my chosen life style undisturbed during my lifetime, regardless of what effect that may have in the lifetimes of my children and grandchildren. Affluence means to acquire an overwhelming and ever-increasing prosperity—a life made up of things, things, and more things—to gain a success which is judged by a continually rising level of material abundance.[6] Apathy doesn't concern itself with others. It only cares about self and materialism!

In the paralysis of fear a person shoots randomly without a target. In the paralysis of anger he wonders why he should shoot at all. Who cares?

Action: Detached

When a person is gripped with the paralysis of anger, apathy results. It's a cover-up for repressed anger and a shield against painful relationships. The only way apathy can stay in operation is by detachment—staying away from any deeper, intimate relationships. Normally, people who live the pressure-cooker life style have few, if any, close relationships. Their life is filled with detached, surface-only relationships. Well-liked by many, they are well known by no one! Any family relationships involved in their life style just add pressure to the cooker because of their inability to make long-term commitments. Obviously, the most critical problem produced by the paralysis of anger is the *lack of relationships*! This problem will be discussed more thoroughly in chapter 13, "The Family—Split and Splintered"!

PARALYSIS OF GUILT—FAITHLESSNESS

Self: Out of Control

True guilt is easily the major cause of all human breakdown, and the feelings of guilt can self-destruct a person faster than anything. That's the nature of guilt—it seeks to punish us for our wrongdoings. The origin of guilt is the philosophical time bomb.[7] Some people think they don't have a problem with guilt because they have everything well in hand. However, that's not an adequate criterion for deciding they have no guilt. Since guilt is a painful feeling, we can unknowingly disguise it and hide it from our conscious minds. By pushing it into the unconscious, we avoid the pain and consider ourselves free from it. But our restless emotional lives betray us, for we continue to be troubled by inner conflicts and frustrations as the repressed guilt sneaks out under other names.[8]

In spite of our "enlightened society," our "new morality," and our "psychological maturity," we are still plagued by guilt. Granted we have disguised it as guilt, but all we have actually done is to substitute a new vocabulary and a new code for it. Parents and teachers who used to say a child was "good" or "bad" now say he is "mature" or "immature," and "adjusted" or "maladjusted." What we feel if we aren't "mature" or "well-adjusted" is still that old sense of guilt. Thus, in a world plagued by personal frustrations and attended by an army of mental health professionals, many people are looking for relief from a nameless anxiety without realizing their basic problem is really guilt.[9]

The paralysis of guilt is all too real. It has put man out of control—in rebellion, estrangement, isolation, and alienation. His performance is in error; he is missing the mark (the old Hebrew meaning). But what is the standard by which man can measure himself? How can he know when he's in or out of control? What is he in rebellion against, in estrangement, isolation, or alienation from? Where is his performance in error, and what is the mark he is missing? If there is no standard of morality or universal "should" then there is no guilt. And if there is no guilt, then who has pulled off this guilt-trip hoax that every civilization from time immemorial has experienced? What a con job! The problem with the "hoax" theory is that no matter what it's called some sense of "should" gnaws away at people and eventually disintegrates their personness. The paralysis of guilt continues to immobilize and destroy. Therefore, the search for a standard will go on, and the moral questions of right and wrong will continue.

Is there an objective morality that has claims on all men, or must we constantly be constructing our own individual, situational moralities? Victor Frankl comments on the despair of youth today who find themselves in what he calls an existential vacuum: "Each person is the center of his own universe . . . there is a denial that there are any claims which come from 'without' himself." All morality in this vacuum is subjective. If this is true, if all morality is purely subjective, then there are almost 3 billion such "moralities" in the world today—3 billion people denying there are any objective principles governing the relatedness between people and going their own way. Yet the fact is the search for objective principles and the longing for relatedness is a universal reality. It is also a personal, experiential reality. The fact is that people cannot and do not want to live unrelated to other people.[10]

If there is no standard of morality then we are left with absurdity! For example, if there is no universal "should," there is no basis for saying Albert Schweitzer was a better man than Adolf Hitler. The only valid observation we may make is that Albert Schweitzer did such and so and Adolf Hitler did such and so. Even though we might make further notations that Albert Schweitzer saved an unknown number of lives while Adolf Hitler slaughtered millions, those facts would only be statistical markings on a page of history and would have no relevance to any ethical reflection about human behavior. After all, the worth of people cannot be proven scientifically. Albert Schweitzer thought he was right and Adolf Hitler thought he was right. That they were both right is an obvious contradiction. *But by what standard do we determine who was right? Without a standard, man is out of control!*[11]

Disease of Dissatisfaction

Dissatisfaction reigns in our society! Whether it's with the future, relationships, or self, the primary dissatisfaction caused by the paralysis of guilt is inside a person—with who he is and why he is! This underlying dissatisfaction is clearly explained by Dr. Karl Menninger, acting director of the Menninger Psychiatric Clinic in Topeka, Kansas, one of the most well known and highly respected centers for the study and practice of psychiatry in America:

> Many centuries have passed since the Hebrew seers preached the importance of a moral code—preached and warned and exhorted and died. Human beings have become more numerous but scarcely more moral. They are busy, coming and going, getting and begetting, fighting and defending, creating and destroying. Many move about now, very swiftly, very far, and in large groups and small. Their numbers have multiplied vastly, spreading over former deserts, forests, and wilderness. They have learned how to cover the grass with pavement, wash the soil and refuse into the ocean, and besmear the earth with waste. They now communicate with one another in a thousand ways, swift and slow; they transport themselves rapidly on land, sea, and through the air. They also *fail* to communicate in a thousand ways and continue to destroy one another with great effectiveness. They spend most of their wealth on stockpiles of explosives and poisons.
> Many of them live lives of great comfort and ease while

other thousands die of starvation daily. Millions, barely surviving, exist most miserably, working at monotonous drudgery. Conscripts are coerced to hurl fire, poisons, and explosives at "enemies" whom they resemble but do not know, and have only fictitious reasons for fearing or hating. Those not at war engage in angry dissensions over property, priorities, privilege, policy, and popularity. Fear and uncertainty, even among the prosperous, lead many citizens to rearm themselves with privately owned killing machines, as in earlier days (but with more deadly weapons).

It became the epoch of technology, rampant and triumphant. We boasted of our inventions, innovations, and gadgets. Rugged individualism, acquisition, thrift, boldness, and shrewdness were acclaimed as the great national virtues. Although hard work was admired, luxury and ease were inordinately esteemed. And as we appropriated and accumulated, we bragged and we braved.

Noisy display enticed people in less prosperous countries to rush to our shores and join in the great grab. These newcomers were exploited in order to produce more and more "gross national products" and electrical energy. We dammed up more and more rivers and gouged out more coal and smashed down more forests. Our population increased—too much. Our traffic increased—much too much. Everything was "going great"—but too much.

Suddenly we awoke from our pleasant dreams with a fearful realization that *something was wrong*.[12]

That which is wrong is the disease of dissatisfaction! In an age of unparalleled progress, man remains in quiet desperation on the gut-level.

Action: Inhuman

The human disease of dissatisfaction has moved man to search for other means of action, ones which are inhuman. He acts like an animal, a machine, a vibration, a computer, a nonman, and so on—anything but human, where he has previously experienced such pain and dissatisfaction! But these other means of action are not true to life as it is and people as they are! None of them fit the human experience! Thus the creation of another critical problem—*the lack of reality*! (Inhuman action and the lack of reality will be discussed in chapter 14—"The Rape of Personness.")

TIME BOMBS	LEVELS of DISINTEGRATION	OUT of CONTROL	DISEASE	ACTION	LACK
(Physical) ┃ (Metaphysical) Ecological ┃ Psychological Chemical ┃ Religious Biological ┃ Parapsychological ─────────── (Regulators Political ┃ Educational	Paralysis of Fear	Future	Destination Sickness	Instant	Responsibility
Sociological	Paralysis of Anger	People	Apathy	Detached	Relationship
Philosophical	Paralysis of Guilt	Self	Dissatisfaction	Inhuman	Reality

Cycle of Disintegration—Forward and Reverse

If the cycle of disintegration always moved in the same direction, it wouldn't be so difficult to stop. But, of course, it doesn't! The cycle not only whirls in two directions but it can start anywhere:

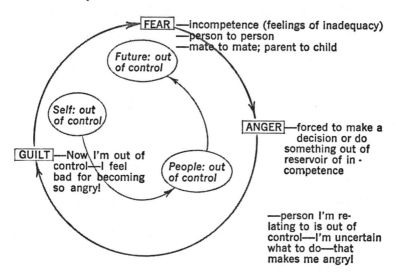

The reverse direction is also prevalent. The paralysis of guilt with all of its dissatisfaction makes a person unhappy, and his unhappiness then produces anger. Guilt and anger combine to stir up fear. If a person can't control himself or his relationships, then how will he ever be able to control the overwhelming and frightening future?

Utopia—Is It Eutopia or Outopia?

Eutopia is the Greek word for "good place" and *outopia* is Greek for "no place." Which will it be?

In his book, *Future Shock*, Alvin Toffler puts the challenge this way: "If man's 50,000 years on this planet are divided into lifetimes of approximately 62 years, then there have been 800 such lifetimes. Of these, over 600 were spent in caves, only the last 70 have had written communication, and only the last 6 have had printed words. But of them all the most crucial is our lifetime—the 800th. This one lifetime is the center of history with as much happening in it as in all the previous lifetimes put together .... Unless man quickly learns to control the rate of change in his personal affairs as well as in society at large, we are doomed to a massive adaptational breakdown .... *This breakdown is future shock.*"[13]

Future shock may usher us into "no place"!

Our lives are shaped by those who love us—by those who refuse to love us.

John Powell

I am nowhere a somewhatness for anyone.

Buddhagosa

All the things that family provided can now be provided outside the family—sexual gratification, companionship, friendship, economic support, even procreation . . . the family served its purpose once, but today it is a very disruptive, destructive system. . . .

F. M. Esfandiary

13

The Family—Split and Splintered

A PSYCHIATRIST WAS ASKED, "How can you teach people to love?" He answered the question by asking a couple of his own: "Have you ever had a toothache? Who were you thinking about while your tooth was aching?" He made his point. When we are in pain, even if it is only the passing discomfort of a toothache, we are thinking about ourselves.

The psychiatrist continued: "This is a pain-filled world in which we are living. And the pains that reside deep in the human hearts around us are not like toothaches. We go to bed with them at night and we wake up with them in the morning. . . . This is a pain-filled world, and so, a loveless world that we live in. Most human beings are so turned-in by their own pains that they cannot get enough out of themselves to love to any great extent."[1]

When a person is *paralyzed* by fear, anger, and guilt, *weakened* by destination sickness, apathy, and dissatisfaction, and *overwhelmed* by his out-of-control world, the family unit is the first to break down under the pressure! Many believe that as the family is built up or broken down, society as a whole follows it.

157

The family is society's "giant shock absorber"—the place where bruised and battered individuals can retreat and rest after doing battle with the world, the one stable point in the ever erratic environment. But, the superindustrial revolution has unfolded and exploded its time bombs, the "giant shock absorber" has been getting some shocks of its own.[2]

The family cycle has been a major sanity-preserving constant throughout human existence and especially since the mass society has evolved. Today this cycle is accelerating, people grow up sooner, leave home sooner, marry sooner, and have children sooner. They space their children closer together and shorten their time of parenthood. In the words of Dr. Bernice Neugarten, a University of Chicago specialist on family development, "The trend is toward a more rapid rhythm of events through most of the family cycle." But if industrialism, with its faster pace of life, has accelerated the family cycle, superindustrialism now threatens to run it aground.[3]

Plan A—A Strategy for Splitting and Splintering!

Most families begin with a marriage, and the dynamics of the marital relationship then set the pace and create the atmosphere for the family to come. Unfortunately, the vast majority of marriages today are caught up in Plan A, which isn't really a plan at all! The theme of this nonplan is offered often, and free of charge, by well-meaning friends and neighborhood marriage counselors: "It'll all work out!" It sounds easy enough! The only catch is—*it doesn't work!* Plan A is based upon a competitive and comparative struggle which revolves around the question, "Who is more qualified here, you or me?"

Man: Dictator in Retreat

When the man first asks himself this question, his initial response is, "Well, *I* am. *I* call most of the shots around here!" Then one day he gets off work early and arrives home during the pit hour (from 4:30 p.m. until the children are in bed—I call it the "valley of the shadow")! With the kids screaming, the bath water running, and dinner somewhere in between, he begins to feel incapable of exerting a controlling influence over the situation. Now he's not so sure about his shots. His wife seems to be surviving and all he seems to be is ready to return to the office.

The man has heard the rumor that he's supposed to be the "head of the home" (whatever that means). So one day he arrives home and announces to his family, "I am the head!" His wife doesn't believe him, the kids don't bat an eye, and not even the dog barks back! Having received such an overwhelming vote, the man retreats! However, the rumor is so prevalent that he returns—and once again makes his announcement—this time with more hesitancy: "I *am* the head! Aren't I? How about when you're out shopping? Could I be the head, *then?*" Now he's thoroughly confused!

Because of his confusion about what his responsibility should be in the home, the man decides to retreat to his office. In a sense, he marries his business! Here's how he does it: "Honey, I'll take care of the business, and you take care of the home. I'll deposit, you can withdraw, and if I can deposit more than you can withdraw—or quicker than you can withdraw—then we will have a dynamic marital relationship!"

Not long after the man has retreated from his responsibilities in the home, he begins to resent his wife for taking over in various household matters. He's the one who retreated, all right, but now he resents her and his resentment turns into reaction. During crisis situations he says, "Why didn't you check with me before you did that? Didn't you even think to consult me about this or have you even *had* a thought lately?"

The man is seeking total fulfillment—a full expression of himself as a person. Since he's retreated to the office and now resents his wife for taking over at home, he can't experience this fulfillment or expression with her, so he runs elsewhere— his business and other people then become substitutes for his relationship with his wife! *The husband's retreat from his responsibility in the home is the most severely damaging move toward splitting and splintering the family.* The most harmful result of his retreat is that the wife is left to absorb all of his pressures in the home—alone! The Plan A wife becomes:

Woman: Doormat in Residence

The woman has heard a rumor too! She's heard that she is supposed to be her husband's "helpmate." However, this concept is normally presented "helpmate" equals doormat! So the Plan A wife is out to prove herself more qualified than a doormat! This brings about all kinds of excitement and provides for all kinds of entertainment in the Plan A home! It becomes a two-ring circus. The man is announcing himself as the head and the woman is trying to prove herself more qualified than a doormat!

The woman's first response to the man's retreat from the home is to release him from his responsibilities there (he's just in the way most of the time, anyway). However, as the pressures build up, she begins to resent her husband for not being there when she needs him. Her reaction during crisis situations is, "Where were you when I needed you? If you'd only be the man of the house, this kind of thing would never happen!"

Just like the man, the woman is seeking total fulfillment—a full expression of herself as a person! She certainly isn't experiencing a full expression of herself with her husband. In fact, it seems more like a full suppression, so she runs elsewhere—to her children, to women's activities, to a vocation, to anywhere away from the relationship!

The marital dynamics (or lack of them) in the Plan A home are primarily responsible for reproducing the relationship dynamics of the next generation. Because the primary victim of Plan A is the child, many believe the chaotic Plan A life style may be the source of the delinquent!

Child: Delinquent in the Rough?

The principal base of security for a child is not derived from dad and mom's love for the child, but from dad and mom's love for each other! In a Plan A home that base of security just isn't there. Everyone's too busy keeping score to have the time or energy to cultivate their love together.

Following the model of his parents, the child quickly becomes a pro in competitive and comparative relationships. Each family member is on his own, because his parents have refused to communicate with each other. Each is out for his/ her own! The child then refuses to communicate with them. He'll communicate about necessary and surface things like "Pass the butter," "May I have some money, mom?" or "Could you take me to the game?" But rarely will he communicate on the gut-level and share what he's thinking or feeling on the inside.

A noncommunicative relationship inevitably brings about resentment and rebellion! Parents usually react to this rebellion with a new list of regulations, and yet even though that's the most natural response, it also turns out to be the most disastrous! More regulations without a healthy relationship only produce more rebellion!

As soon as he can, the child runs elsewhere, from an insecure base at home to an even more insecure society. He's searching for the fulfillment he missed in his family relationships. He's out to fill up all the gaps and vacuums he senses inside and he'll try it all until he finds something that fits!

A noticeable characteristic of a Plan A family is that nobody's home! You can call there day or night and never get an answer! Everyone is continually rushing here and there, and with all the coming and going the home simply becomes a local motel! It's because those living there have discovered that relationships are avoided, not developed, because those living there have discovered that relationships are too painful.

There is a process whereby a person learns to avoid relationships:

As a child I realize that people:

get impatient with me	reject me
blame me	hurt me
yell at me	deceive me

lecture me	punish me
won't listen to me	

A door slams shut inside me. *My inner voice says:*

love hurts	I don't need your love
I can't trust love or big	I won't ask for love
people	

I erect barriers:

I am afraid	I become aggressive and
I am inferior	hostile
I become critical	I withdraw

I search for people to meet my needs:

business colleagues	a husband/wife
special acquaintances	a close friend
special interest groups	a substitute parent

If people fail me, I seek substitutes:

physical appearance	intelligence
sex appeal	degrees
security	titles
money	abilities
achievement	recognition
honors	

Plan A—The Shaky Percentages

The family structure has become pretty shaky! Thirty-eight percent of all first marriages fail, 79 percent of those will remarry, and 44 percent of those will divorce again. As many as 4 out of 10 children born in the 1970s will spend part of their childhood in a single-parent family, usually with the mother as head of the household. Seventeen percent of all children under 18 are now living in single-parent families.

One of the most distressing developments in the family structure is the high tide of illegitimacy. Fifteen percent of all births are illegitimate, and more than half of all out-of-wedlock babies are born to teenagers. Illegitimacy was particularly high among black women in 1976—50.3 percent bore illegitimate children. These illegitimate children, both black and white, are the ones most likely to be impoverished, dependent on welfare, deprived of educational opportunities, and destined to repeat the cycle with illegitimate children of their own.[5]

The Plan A Home: Enter at Your Own Risk

A study by the University of Rhode Island described the American home as the most dangerous place to be, outside of riots and war! Although exact statistics are difficult to obtain, all the other available studies have echoed the same sad story. The Plan A home is filled with anger and violence! Thirty percent of all American couples experience some form of domestic violence in their lifetime, and two million couples have used a gun, knife, or other lethal weapon on each other during their marriage. Twenty percent of all police officers killed in the line of duty are killed while answering calls involving family fights, and it's estimated that anywhere from 6 to 15 million women are battered in the United States each year! As one law officer expressed it: "This is probably the highest unreported crime in the country."[6]

Plan A—An Optical Problem: The Big "I"

"Every age develops its own peculiar forms of pathology, which express in exaggerated form its underlying character structure," writes social critic Christopher Lasch. He and others have said that ours is an age of narcissism, recalling the Greek legend about the beautiful youth who fell in love with his reflection in a pool and pined away in rapture over it.[7]

Narcissism is a combination of an exaggerated sense of self-importance and a lack of sustained positive regard for others. A narcissist isn't really in love with himself—self-hatred is more prevalent than self-love. Narcissists actually have low opinions of themselves, and that's why they constantly seek approbation. They consider themselves unworthy and unlovable, so they attempt to hide those feelings by getting the outside world to proclaim them extraordinary or unique. Even then they suffer from intense, unconscious envy that makes them want to degrade, depreciate, and spoil what others have and they lack, particularly others' capacity to love and give. The narcissist is never totally satisfied by what he receives from others, and he usually ends up frustrated and feeling empty.[8]

Incapable of loving themselves, narcissists cannot give to their partners in a relationship. The capacity to fall in love implies the ability to idealize another person. In a sense, all love begins as infatuation. Initially we see the loved one as extraordinary, remarkable, even perfect, but inevitably as the relationship continues things begin to look different and disappointment sets in. When people are in love, they can regenerate the feeling of idealization again and again over a long period of time, but the narcissist can't idealize anyone for very long. As soon as a person the narcissist has idealized responds to him, that person loses his or her value. The narcissist is purely exploitative in his relationships with other people. It's as if he were squeezing a lemon and then dropping the remains.[9]

The narcissistic personality disorder has become such a widespread problem in our society that it's expected to receive official clinical status in the American Psychiatric Association's diagnostic manual in 1980. The proposed description reads:

A. Grandiose sense of self-importance.
B. Preoccupation with fantasies of unlimited success, power, brilliance, beauty, or ideal love.
C. Exhibitionistic: requires constant attention and admiration.
D. Responds to criticism, indifference of others, or defeat with either cool indifference or with marked feelings of rage, inferiority, shame, humiliation, or emptiness.
E. At least two of the following are characteristic of disturbances in interpersonal relationships:
  1. Lack of empathy: inability to recognize how others feel.
  2. Entitlement: expectation of special favors without assuming reciprocal responsibilities.
  3. Interpersonal exploitiveness.

4. Relationships characteristically vacillate between the extremes of overidealization and devaluation.[10]

Do you know anyone like that? It's the "me" generation, and it's a major part of the debris from the time bombs! Psychologist Kenneth Keniston of the Massachusetts Institute of Technology says: "If you live in a society where you believe the public institutions are deeply flawed and not easily improved, that leaves the pursuit of individual happiness in a private way as the main challenge to your energies." Burton Bradley, an Atlanta psychologist, adds: "People are trying to cope with an insane world. The 'me' idea is really more a question of survival than self-indulgence."[11]

Plan A—Multiplies Itself

Plan A families are normally produced by other Plan A families, and they in turn reproduce other Plan A families. We learn how to develop or destroy relationships through our primary models—parents! There's no doubt that the best preparation for building healthy families in the future is to begin now with the parents of the future families!

The challenge is overwhelming! Raising children has never been more costly—in terms of time and money—and interference from the outside has never been more acute. Schools, peer pressure, television, and even the family experts have all invaded the home, robbing parents of much of their power without easing much of their responsibility. "Parents are not abdicating," says MIT psychologist Keniston, "they are being dethroned by forces they cannot influence, much less control." The pressure is intense! "We're the ultimate nuclear family, and sometimes I feel as if someone is trying to split the atom," says Georgia Houser, 35, a Houston college administrator and mother of three. And on occasion, a parent's plight can be sadly ludicrous: a 24-year-old drifter in Colorado sued his parents for $350,000, charging their failure had made him what he is.[12]

Plan A is the most devastating debris from the time bombs affecting relationships today, and it continues to split and splinter the foundation unit of society. Yet even though Plan A doesn't work, it's still the most popular Plan for relationships around. Isn't there another plan? Has anyone suggested that we move on to Plan B?

Most men lead lives of quiet desperation.
Thoreau
In seeking to become angels we may become
less than man.
Pascal
It is becoming more and more obvious, that it is
not starvation, not microbes, not cancer but man
himself who is mankind's greatest danger.
Carl Jung

14

The Rape of Personness

OUT OF CONTROL! The future, people, and the self are all out
of control! However, the basic problem doesn't rest in the future or in our relationships with other people, but in how man
views himself as he faces the future and relates to people! The
problem most critical to mankind is the *nature of man.*

As man comes face to face with himself, even the predictions of the optimists tend to be prepared at some point with
premonitions of disaster; Teilhard de Chardin, for all his
buoyant blitheness, wrote in December 1953, two and a half
years before his death, "Man now sees that the seeds of his
ultimate dissolution are at the heart of his being. *The End of
the Species* is in the marrow of our bones!" Norman O. Brown,
descending momentarily from his rarified romanticism, wrote,
"Today even the survival of humanity is a utopian hope."
Most sobering of all is the Russel-Einstein Manifesto deliv-
ered in 1955 at the Caxton Hall, London, two days before
Albert Einstein died. Outlining the risks of thermonuclear
warfare, it bluntly warned, "We have found that the men who
know are the most gloomy . . . as human beings, to human
beings; remember your humanity and forget the rest. If you

do so, the way lies open to a new Paradise; if you cannot, there lies before you the risk of universal death." [1]

"Remember your humanity"—your personness! All this concern about personness is because there's a crime being committed against the human race! And there is no better description of the crime than rape. Rape is "the act of seizing and carrying off by force" and that is exactly what is occurring. Mankind is being raped of its personness, and as a result man is becoming less than man—man is quickly becoming nonman! Could he become a zero? There are rapists roving about in society seeking to seize man's personness and carry it off by force! Somebody needs to scream RAPE!

Man—Nothing but Molecules?

This rapist carries man's personness off by reducing the explanation of his parts. In other words, man is just a collection of molecules!

To the chemist man is a compilation of chemicals—quite ordinary elements with familiar properties—well-behaved molecules combining regularly and predictably. Some of the combinations are highly complex, but gradually the fascinating story has been told of amino-acids, proteins, enzymes, and even the marvelous double helix of DNA. In 1953 Drs. Francis Crick and James D. Watson announced their discoveries of these intricate molecules which transmit genetic characteristics. Blue eyes, fair hair, and perhaps even the talent for mathematics could all be traced to the nucleic acids on the DNA strands. The miracles of blood, muscle, and nerve can all be reduced to ordered patterns of biochemical laws. Man is a collection of common chemicals—mostly carbon, with a dash of phosphorus, enough iron to make a six-inch nail, and enough sulphur to rid one dog of fleas—put together with about a hundredweight of water. [2]

But where is "man' 'in this collection of molecules? His molecules change completely every seven years or so—and yours are changing in part even as you read this page—so how is "personness" related to this changing molecular pile? [3]

The problem with this rapist is that *meaning* may transcend a *reductionistic description.* The British scientist and philosopher, Donald MacKay, cleverly illustrates this with a neon sign! We can understand the principles of a neon sign—how the filaments work, how the current goes through, how the atoms are broken down into electrons with positive ions going in opposite directions to maintain the beautiful colors—perfectly well without realizing that what it says is "Joe's Bar and Grill." The meaning of the sign is not reducible to the physical chemistry of the neon tubes. Likewise, the meaning of this sentence is not reducible to its letters, even though the letters make up 100 percent of its content.[4]

Jacques Monod, a French Nobel-laureate, wrote a book-length essay entitled "Chance and Necessity." Unexpectedly it zoomed onto the Parisian best-seller list and came in just behind the French translation of Eric Segal's *Love Story.* The thesis of Monod's essay is hardly the kind to move the sentimental or soothe the uncertain. After some 30 years of research in biochemistry and genetics, Monod is convinced that man's existence is due to the chance collision in the vast prebiotic soup of minuscule particles of nucleic acid and proteins. Monod comments on man's response to that—to his feeling like a nonman: "Our number came up at a Monte Carlo game, and like someone who just made $1 million at the tables, this realization makes man feel strange and unreal."[5]

Bertrand Russell, the English philosopher-mathematician, sums up this rape of mankind: "Man's beliefs, are but the outcome of accidental collocations of atoms."[6] *Is that all man is—molecules?*

Man—Nothing but a Machine?

B. F. Skinner, the famous Harvard psychologist, whose voice we heard in "It's All in Your Head" (Chapter 4), is a chief proponent of this rapist—man is only a product of his environment. He's just a stimulus-response machine with no trace of personness!

Skinner and his followers advocate that man is a product

of his surroundings. His behavior is in no way a result of his own decisions or desires, but is totally determined by his outside world. Skinner insists that man's actions are determined by the external environment, that his behavior "is shaped and maintained by its consequences."[7] The behaviorists believe humans are subjects who can be molded at will to a particular pattern of behavior. Like the laboratory animals, they can be conditioned by Skinner's method of reward.

The behaviorists do away with man as a unique creative being, with his inner person, as Skinner says: "What is being abolished is autonomous man—the inner man, the homunculus man, the possessing demon, the man defended by the literatures of freedom and dignity. His abolition has long been overdue. . . . To man *qua* man we readily say good riddance."[8]

Man becomes part of the cosmic machinery! Everything he is, everything he makes, everything he thinks is completely, 100 percent, determined by his environment. "Man" doesn't exist—he's just not there. All that's there is a bundle of conditioning, a genetic code, the past, and the environment. Man is nothing but a machine—raped of his personness![9]

Man—Nothing but an Animal?

Man is raped again! This time unique personness is carried off by reducing him to a biological organism. Undoubtedly he is the best developed of the animals, but he is still a physiological specimen whose primary function is to survive and reproduce.

In the 1960s three or four books were published which assumed that the "real" human nature would be found by examining animal and bird behavior. The "naked ape" is "inescapably hostile and competitive," they said, and even his friendships and loves are rooted in aggression and territory-defense. Anthony Storr really laid it on thick in the introduction to his book, *Human Aggression* (which he dedicated to Konrad Lorenz with "admiration and affection," qualities that must have temporarily outweighed his aggression): "That man is an aggressive creature will hardly be disputed . . . the cruellest and most ruthless species that has ever walked the earth; and that, although we may recoil in horror when we read in newspaper or history book of the atrocities committed by man upon man, we know in our hearts that each one of us harbours within himself those same savage impulses which lead to murder, to torture and to war." There is more than suggestion in all this that aggression, like sexual impulse, is built into the biological structure of humanity, and there is little that can be done about it.[10]

Is man just the apex of the evolutionary process? Is he nothing but an animal? People have been taught this for so long that much of the time they act like animals toward other "animals."

Man = Impersonal + Time + Chance

Man has been raped and left for dead! He becomes simply the product of an impersonal origin with only the addition of the equally impersonal time and chance. He has a genetic code, and he has an environment to shape the product of the code. But that's all he has, and all he is—man is dead.[11]

It's interesting to note the way the rapists of personness inject personness back into their nonperson systems. Dr. Francis Crick says, "You cannot lay down a general trend (for the course of evolution); natural selection is *cleverer* than that. It will *think* of combinations and ways of doing things which haven't been foreseen." Crick's language here attributes to natural selection a sort of personality. In *The Origin of the Genetic Code* (1968) Crick begins to spell Nature with a capital about halfway through the book, and in *Of Molecules and Men* (1967) he calls nature a "she." In other words he personalizes what his own system has defined as impersonal. He does so because he can't stand the implications of impersonality, and this kind of semantic mysticism gives relief to people caught in the web of the impersonal.[12]

Man can't live within the impersonal systems for one very simple reason—his own personness! Personness just doesn't fit within the impersonal! It's like a fish attempting to live out of water, or a train maneuvering through a field without a set of tracks! It just doesn't fit!

Man is a collection of molecules, a stimulus-response machine, a highly developed animal, but he is not only any of these or only a combination of these. Man is something more! When he views himself as just molecules, a machine, or an animal, he becomes extremely frustrated, and dissatisfaction sets in on the gut-level. To avoid being forced into the impersonal mold, which would mean death to him as a man, he then starts striking out against his nature. If man is in an impersonal universe, then the things which make him man— love, hope, rationality, morality, creativity, communication, and choice—are unfulfillable and therefore meaningless. Man becomes as dead as a fish out of water, and as meaningless as a train without a set of tracks!

Man's Ultimate Dilemma: Absolute Relativism

The mood today throughout each of the time bombs is "the only absolute is change." Actually this is a contradiction of terms. If everything is relative then nothing can be absolute! However, it does demonstrate man's lack of a base. There's no basis for right and wrong, no standard by which to measure values, morals, or ethics.

Francis A. Schaeffer, a philosopher-thinker whose brilliant analysis of Western man's development and despair has opened up new perspectives on the meaning of man, discusses the need for absolutes in order to have meaning in life: "Plato did understand something crucial—not only in theoretical thought but in practical life. He saw that if there are no absolutes, then the individual things (the particulars, the details) have no meaning. By particulars we mean the individual things which are about us. The individual stones on a beach are particulars. The molecules are particulars. I am made up of molecules. And I as an individual and you as an individual are particulars.

"Plato understood that regardless of what kind of particulars one talks about, if there are no absolutes—no universal —then particulars have no meaning. The universal or absolute is that under which all the particulars fit—that which gives unity and meaning to the whole. We can apply this in language. Apples come in many varieties, but we do not verbalize each time by running through the names of all the varieties of apples. We sum them up by the word *apples.* Likewise, there are many kinds of pears, and we sum them up with the word *pears.* On a higher level of generality there are many other varieties of fruit. But we again do not run through all these, we simply say *fruit.*

"The problem, however, is not only in language but in reality: What will unify and give meaning to everything there is? Jean-Paul Sartre (1905–), the French existential philosopher, emphasized this problem in our own generation. His concept was that a finite point is absurd if it has no infinite reference point. This concept is most easily understood in the area of morals. If there is no absolute moral standard, then one cannot say in a final sense that anything is right or wrong. By *absolute* we mean that which always applies, that which provides a final or ultimate standard. There must be an absolute if there are to be *morals,* and there must be an absolute if there are to be real *values.* If there is no absolute beyond man's ideas, then there is no final appeal to judge between individuals and groups whose moral judgments conflict. We are merely left with conflicting opinions.

"But it is not only that we need absolutes in morals and values; we need absolutes if our existence is to have *meaning*— my existence, your existence, Man's existence."[13]

The dilemma of people without absolutes is best illustrated by the "rights" explosion of the special interest groups in America. The word "right" was once defined and used for a legal claim on an area of individual discretion, such as freedom of speech, or a limitation on the power of government. Today, it's used for virtually any demand one group makes on another. The smaller and more single-minded the group, the more rights they seem to receive! The term "right" now has an arbitrary definition and arbitrary standards produce fragmentation and conflict.

A Question in Search of an Answer

Three thousand years ago, the psalmist asked, "What is man?" and that same old question is now back in the center of discussion. However, the intervening 3,000 years have seen a lot of discovery and a lot of confusion. Twentieth-century natural and social sciences have become vast, intricate systems of thought, and philosophers have developed countless theories and counter-theories. The small agricultural community of the psalmist has given way to the jungle of the city and the extraordinary complexity of commerce and industry.[14]

The Munich comedian Karl Vallentin was famous for a skit which very cleverly, and clearly, illustrates the folly of contemporary man's search for answers. Coming onto the stage in almost total darkness, with one solitary circle of light provided by a street lamp, he paced around and around the lamp with a long, worried face, as if looking for something. Soon a policeman crossed the stage and asked him what he had lost. Vallentin answered that he had lost the key to his house. The policeman joined in the hunt, but after a while the search appeared fruitless. "Are you sure you lost it here?" asked the policeman. "Oh no!" said Vallentin, pointing to the dark corner, "I lost it over there." "Then why on earth are you looking over here?" asked the policeman. "Because there's no light over there!" replied Vallentin.[15]

The rape of personness forces man to search for meaning in a small lighted area where there is no answer!

Part Three

The Defusing
of the Time Bombs
(How to give yourself
a mental!)

The *detonation* of the time bombs is overwhelming . . . . The *debris* from the time bombs is devastating . . . . The *defusing* of the time bombs is essential to preserving your personness!

The time bombs are defused by giving yourself a mental checkup. A physical check-up is commonly recommended, but since the root cause of most physical problems is in the mind, why not a mental? (Chapter 15 will define the mental. Chapters 16–19 will delineate how it works.)

15
Personness—Like a Fleet of Ships

IN ORDER TO GIVE YOURSELF a mental, you have to know what a mentally healthy "you" looks like. C. S. Lewis, the Cambridge scholar and author, described mental health as being *like a fleet of ships*. In such a fleet (1) each ship has to be seaworthy, (2) the ships can't run into one another, and (3) they must all be going in the same direction. This is a vivid picture of what personness is all about, and it lays out the essential ingredients to a healthy "you." To ignore any one of them is to experience and express less of your personness.

Personness: From Disintegration to Integration

The three levels of disintegration—fear, anger, guilt—are counteracted by one of the ingredients of personness. *The first ingredient is a sense of destiny—hope—which counteracts the paralysis of fear.* (The ships must all be going in the same direction.) A sense of destiny is a sense of direction in life, a sense that you are going somewhere and doing something significant and worthwhile! With a sense of destiny, the future is no longer out of control. There is hope!

Underlying this hope is a personness need to make things

happen instead of waiting for them to happen. It's the need to be an *actor* rather than a reactor! The physical, metaphysical, and regulator time bombs have geared our technological, instant, destination-sick society toward making people react as machines or animals and not as people with personness.

Mental Maxim #2
You can live life by chance circumstances, others' choices, or your choice.

When you are involved in a healthy context of relationships, you have a stronger motivation to be an actor rather than a reactor toward the future. In other words, *love*—a healthy context of relationships, encourages hope—a sense of destiny. But hope and love find their ultimate meaning in the third ingredient of personness.

The third ingredient is a basis for right and wrong—faith—which counteracts the paralysis of guilt (each ship has to be sea-worthy). You have a personness need to base your life on a standard whereby you can measure and evaluate right and wrong and good and bad. This standard or base must be true to life as it is and people as they are! And without this base you are stuck with your feet firmly planted in midair! It's the personness need to have a game-plan for your life! Not a box —but a game-plan!

Faith is the game-plan for right and wrong which counteracts guilt. *Love* is the dynamic of relationships which counteracts anger. *Hope* is the sense of destiny about the future which counteracts fear. These ingredients can transform your personness from disintegration into integration!

Mental Maxim #3
Personness can't happen in a relationship vacuum.

The first ingredient of personness, a sense of destiny—hope —rests and depends upon the second. *The second ingredient is*

*a healthy context of relationships—love—which counteracts
the paralysis of anger* (the ships can't run into one another).
You have a personness need to love and be loved. It's all too
easy to feel alone in the crowded universe, and in a society
filled with cold detachment, the warmth of healthy relationships is essential to the dynamic of personness. There's an intense need to care for someone and to know someone cares
for you! True personness is discovered within intimate relationships!

PERSONNESS

Levels of Disintegration	Levels of Integration
(Unhealthy "You")	(Healthy "You")
Paralysis of Fear	Hope (Sense of destiny)
Paralysis of Anger	Love (Healthy context of relationships)
Paralysis of Guilt	Faith (Basis for right and wrong)

Personness = Life Processes

The three ingredients of personness are also three processes
of living—*achieving, relating,* and *becoming.* There is no arrival point in life, and those who spend their lives trying to
arrive only bring premature death to their personness. To be
alive and healthy is to be in process. There are no shortcuts!

> *Mental Maxim #4*
> A shortcut is the longest distance between two points.

Personness = Life's Priorities

Priorities don't necessarily refer to quantity of time, but rather to quality of time. First a person must know and understand who he is—*self-reality*. Then he can give himself to cultivating his *intimate relationships*. How successful he is at fulfilling his *vocational/community responsibilities* is then affected by what he thinks of himself and how he relates to his intimate relationships.

There are three *Mental Maxims* that help in understanding the major issues of priorities.

Mental Maxim #5
Things get worse under pressure.

It's bad enough without the pressure! Priorities enable you to relieve much of the pressure in your life, because they let you take control of yourself, your relationships, and your future. Priorities put you in the driver's seat!

Mental Maxim #6
Priorities are not the arrival-point but the process for arriving at a point!

The most common misconception about priorities is that once you establish them, you will arrive in complete control of your life. But because life's priorities are also subject to processes, just like the ingredients of personness, that isn't true. On Monday you organize your life according to your priorities, but since the process of living goes beyond Monday, the process of controlling your life by the use of priorities must continue on Tuesday and Wednesday and Thursday, and so on. To reach the arrival point is a literal living end! *You can't arrive and stay alive!*

Priorities offer guidelines or levels of long-term importance. In the long term your intimate relationships are more important than your vocational/community responsibilities, but your self-reality is even more important than your intimate relationships. Now there's a magic word that makes priorities work. It's *"No!"* Either most people have no idea when to say it, or they just don't have the heart to say it. However, when these priorities come into conflict, a confident and not at all heartless "No!" can be given to the lesser priority. Priorities are not just a silly game. They're a game-plan which enables you to skillfully orchestrate your life toward a more fully expressed personness. It's a process of taking control of your life style for the "best."

Mental Maxim #7
The "good" is the greatest enemy of the "best."

Without a doubt the most successful enemy of the "best" is the "good." It's easy to say "No!" when you really *want* to say "No"—when you don't want to do something. The difficult "No!" comes when you want to say "Yes," when you want to do something. That "No!" hurts! But you can't do everything you want to, not even when it's all "good." There's barely enough time for the "best" as it is. Your "No!" is just as important to your mental health as your "Yes!"

PERSONNESS	PROCESSES	PRIORITIES
Hope	Achieving	Vocational Community Responsibility
Love	Relating	Intimate Relationships
Faith	Becoming	Self Reality

Mental Checkup—A Way of Seeing

The mental checkup is not a box to live in, a program to follow, or emotional hype to put you on top of the pile! It's a way of seeing! It's a grid for seeing and evaluating your self, your relationships, and your destiny on a long-term basis. But even while viewing life on a long-term basis, the mental will help you keep your feet planted firmly in the base of reality.

Mental Maxim #8

Reality isn't the way you wish things to be, nor the way they appear to be, but the way they actually are.

If you don't acknowledge reality and use it to your benefit, it will inevitably work against you. You have the choice of either employing it on your behalf, or allowing it to beat you over the head. Those who take control of reality are realists. *A realist is a person who believes in basing his life on facts and who dislikes anything that seems imaginary, impractical, theoretical, or utopian.*[1]

The most common problem in becoming a realist is your wishing ability—whether it's wishing for what you like or against what you dislike. The "ether" of wishing can blind you from seeing reality! Simply stated by Ayn Rand, ". . . facts cannot be altered by a wish, but they *can* destroy the wisher."[2]

Mental Maxim #9

If there's not a picture on the puzzle, the pieces are meaningless!

Mental Checkup—Way of Thinking

As you give yourself a mental, you are forced to think! Thinking is the process of getting the picture so you can put the pieces together. It's expanding your perspective on life so you can know how it all fits together. The wider your perspective becomes, the wiser your decisions will be.

A wider perspective also tends to let the steam out of pressurized situations. Now, if you're in Hiroshima and it's 1945, you have a problem worthy of considerable concern, and one worth worrying about! But if you've recently been chiseled in a business deal, or your child announced last week that he hates you, or the bank notified you this morning that you're overdrawn, I'm sure you find a way to survive, by calming down, reviewing the situation, and thinking it through.

Is middle age depressing you? Some people aren't bothered by such things. In parts of the world where the average life expectancy is thirty-seven years, men and women are spared the distressing experience of a fortieth birthday party. *Are grocery bills getting you down?* More than 10,000 people die of starvation every day, while millions more suffer from malnutrition. *Sick of the high cost of rent?* Maybe you'd rather be a pavement dweller in Calcutta. Those lucky stiffs are born, live, and die on the pavement. The only thing they have to worry about is finding a rag to spread under their heads at night.[3]

While these kinds of horrors continue along at their normal, accepted pace, we throw tantrums over being seated at a poorly located table in a fancy restaurant, are frustrated because we can't seem to lose weight, and gripe endlessly about monthly bills. You've got problems? Relative to what?[4]

With a mental way of thinking you can widen the perspective on your problems rather than pressure-cook them inside your person!

Mental Checkup Defined

The mental checkup is a way of seeing and thinking about life's processes and priorities. The result is the unique expression of your personness! *By giving yourself a mental, you can experience a realistic, relational, and responsible life style!*

16

You Can't Fall Off the Floor

MENTAL CHECKUP

STEP ONE: CHOOSE A REALISTIC BASE!

YOUR PERSONNESS NEEDS to be built on an adequate base of reality. This base must be strong enough to support all you are and secure enough so you can't fall off! What you need is a floor! You can fall off walls, balconies, buildings, swings, bridges, cliffs, or out of the air! *But you can't fall off the floor!*

True to People As They Are and Life As It Is!

The bottom line for choosing a realistic base is to find one that's true to people as they are and life as it is! The philosopher Jean-Paul Sartre said the basic philosophic question is that something is there rather than that nothing is there. It's difficult to deny the existence of people as they are—they have *personness,* and life as it is—it has *universals.* The base you choose must be true to personness and universals.

To explain how to choose a realistic base, I think it may be helpful to use the base I chose as an example. Naturally, I think I made the best choice for my personness and the universals which make my particulars most meaningful, but my motive is simply to make you *think* about my choice as you search for your own realistic base. It's none of my business whether you buy it or not! I feel like the Toyota commercial that said: "If you can find a better car than Toyota, you'd better buy it!" I agree: "If you can find a better base than mine, you'd better buy it!" But no matter what you think of my chosen base, you must choose a realistic base for yourself!

I began giving myself a mental about eight years ago, and I chose a 1730-page book as my realistic base. It's entitled *Bible*!

After digging through all the versions and perversions of that book, I found it to be an adequate base for personness and universals.

Mental Maxim #11
It works better if you plug it in!

People work better if they are plugged in to a personness base! But what is the base of personness? Where did man's personness come from? There are only three possibilities.

Man Came from Nothing

The first possibility is that all existence (people as they are) came out of *nothing!* Now, to hold this view, it must be *absolutely* nothing. It can't be nothing something or something nothing. It must be nothing nothing, which means there must be no energy, no mass, no motion, and no personality. Practically, this option is unthinkable! But theoretically, it's the first possible answer.[1]

Man Came from Impersonal

The second possibility is that all existence came from an *impersonal* beginning! The impersonality could be mass, energy, motion, or a combination of things, but they would all be equally impersonal. If an impersonal beginning is accepted, some form of reductionism always follows. Everything, from the stars to man himself, is finally understood by reducing it to the original, impersonal factor or factors—just mass, energy, motion, or whatever.[2]

The biggest problem in beginning with the impersonal is to find meaning for the particulars. If we begin with the impersonal, then how do any of the particulars now existing—including man—have any meaning, any significance? Beginning with the impersonal, everything, including man, must be explained in terms of the impersonal plus time plus chance.[3]

The impersonal base is commonly called *naturalism*. Naturalism holds that everything can be explained by the natural laws of the universe. All existence and its operation is confined to this closed system, and nothing exists or operates outside of it. In other words, all existence is one big cosmic machine, and it includes people as they are. Man finds himself caught in it—in fact, he is only a cog in the machine!

Naturalism is the base for humanism, and humanism is the base for the bankruptcy of personness. The dilemma of modern humanism and the reason for the declaration of bankruptcy is simple. It's matter plus time plus chance equals zero! If man is the illegitimate offspring of a thoughtless parent order, the mockery of fortuitous chance, his significance is nil. Add to this man's inhumanity to man, and the dilemma is intensified. As the humanist is faced with this, his dreams come to wreckage and ruin, and his hopes for a utopian future are shattered!

There isn't an exit from the closed system of naturalism, from the dilemma of humanism. Even man's gods are part of the closed system and therefore incapable of an adequate base for providing personness or universals. Life is a dead-end street! Samuel Beckett, a playwright in the theater of the "absurd," wrote of this trapped position: "How am I, an a-temporal being imprisoned in time and space, to escape from my imprisonment, when I know that outside space and time lies Nothing, and that I, in the ultimate depths of my reality, am Nothing also?"[4]

Man Came from Personal

The third possibility is that all existence came from a *personal* beginning. With a personal beginning as well as the impersonal beginning everything happens according to the natural laws of the universe. But instead of it happening in a closed system (naturalism), it happens in an open system (supernaturalism). In other words, all existence is not one big cosmic machine, and people as they are don't have to be included in it. In an open system, there is something "outside" the cosmic machinery—outside the uniformity of the natural laws—something *super*natural. This "something" outside the natural system is normally called God (as in the biblical base). Because supernaturalism is an open and personal system, the God of the Bible is an adequate base for *personness*—because he is personal—and as a *universal* base for all the particulars —because he is outside of them.

There is no place in the naturalistic, impersonal beginning for man and his personness or God as a universal. But in the supernatural, personal beginning there is hope! Things go on according to the sequence of natural laws, but at any point in time they may be changed by God or by people. Consequently, *there is a place for God's universals and man's personness. This supernatural, personal beginning is an adequate base for personness (true to people as they are) and for universals (true to life as it is).*

BASE FOR UNIVERSALS
(true to life as it is)

The same base which is adequate for your personness is also adequate for universals, which give meaning to people (particulars). After much investigation I chose the Bible as my realistic base. My reasons are outlined in an appendix— "The Supernatural Factor." I've found that once a base is chosen, a person must then begin a search for the universals —the principles of life—that govern how he can live most successfully!

Principles of life are true no matter what you think or believe about them. They're like the laws of nature. For instance, there is the principle of gravity. Stated simply, this principle says if you jump off a two-story building, you'll come down fast and hit with a thud. And you probably won't like it! It doesn't make any difference what you think or believe about it—or whether or not you like it. The principle is true. Even if the principle of gravity was placed on a national ballot and voted down unanimously, the next person who attempted to jump off a two-story building would find the principle didn't know it had been voted out of existence. As he jumped, he would come down fast, and hit with a thud. And he probably wouldn't like it!

When you follow the principle of life, you'll experience personal fulfillment. But if you ignore these principles, you'll experience everything *but* personal fulfillment.

You don't *have* to understand life's principles to follow them. I don't understand how electricity works, but I flip the switch and read by the light. I don't understand how a *brown* cow can eat *green* grass, and make white milk and yellow butter, but I eat all of it—except the grass! Principles are true no matter what level of understanding you have of them.

The principles of life can govern your life toward maximum fulfillment of who you are! There are principles of life style that relate to you alone, to you and your relationships, and to you and your vocation. These principles of life go along with the processes and priorities of personness discussed earlier.

I have an incredible privilege in life. My vocation is to search for the universal principles of life and then speak about them all over the world—to make people think!

On a flight from New York to Los Angeles, an executive sat down beside me. After a few conversational clichés, he asked, "What do you do?"

I quickly replied, "I speak."

He said, "I know that, but what do you do for a living?"

Again I said, "I speak!"

"On what?" he continued.

"Well, I speak on life style, marriage, parenting, long-term selling and managing, and so on."

He seemed interested. "Really! Are you a psychiatrist?"

"No," I replied, "but I have a psychiatrist who works with me."

"Well then," he said, "are you a psychologist?"

"No, I'm not one of those either, but I do have two of them who work for me."

Then in a somewhat frustrated manner he said, "Well, what are you?" Now it hurts a little bit when someone asks *"What are you?"*, but I bounced back with, "I'm just a speaker!" Now that my profession was established, he started on his second set of twenty questions!

"Where do you get your material?"

I told him he probably wouldn't believe me if I told him.

"No," he said, "come on, where do you get your stuff?"

So I told him, "I get it out of a book."

"In a book! What's the title of the book?" he asked.

I had him get out his pen. He fumbled for a minute and finally got his pen and datebook in hand to receive the title of my resource book.

Calmly I announced, "The title of the book is *Bible*."

He seemed a little stunned with my answer and said in a rather loud voice, *"Bible!* You get your material to speak to corporations from the *Bible?* What is there to talk about in the *Bible?"*

I'd heard that question so many times in similar situations, I was ready for it. "Oh," I said, "I speak quite a bit on sex!"

He choked slightly, "From the *Bible?"* His shock came from a common misconception that the *Bible* says, "Thou shalt not!" about sex. It actually says "Thou shalt!" and it even goes so far as to say, "Thou shalt enjoy it, when thou shalt!"

"Oh, yes, from the Bible!" I assured him. "There are all kinds of principles of life concerning sex in the Bible! Moses wrote in Deuteronomy 24:5 that when a man gets married, he shouldn't be drafted into the military or work, but he should *cheer up* his wife for a year! I can't explain it all right now, but that Hebrew word for 'cheer up' doesn't mean to tell jokes for a year. It's referring to sex!"

Now the inquisitive executive began to take notes. "Now, where is that verse?" Can't you just see him going to his hotel room and pulling out the Gideon Bible from the nightstand drawer! Principles of life are universal principles, and no matter where you find them, people want them. That's because they are true to people as they are and life as it is!

The first step in giving yourself a mental is to *choose a realistic base*. It's none of my business what you choose or where you find it, but it must be true to people as they are (a base for personness) and life as it is (a base for universals)!

I found such a base in a book—*Bible*! If you can find a better base than mine, you'd better buy it!

17

You Need the Eggs

MENTAL CHECKUP

STEP TWO: CULTIVATE LOVE RELATIONSHIPS!

ONE OF THE BEST STATEMENTS made concerning relationships
in the 1970s was Woody Allen's award-winning film, *Annie
Hall*. Its message was: relationships are difficult, painful,
and much of the time they seem irrational. But you still need
them. Woody Allen concluded his film by telling the story
about the man who thought he was a chicken. His wife went
to a psychiatrist for some help in dealing with her husband's
problem. After she had explained her husband's behavior to
the doctor he said, "That's ridiculous! Why don't you tell him
he's not a chicken?" The woman immediately responded, "Because I need the eggs!" *Relationships are difficult, but "you
need the eggs" for your personness!*

The second step in giving yourself a mental is to *cultivate
love relationships!* As you build upon your realistic base,
your context of relationships becomes the primary place of
your own personal growth. If you were to draw your lifeline
along a horizontal time line—and make the lifeline go above

191

the horizontal time line during growth periods and below it during nongrowth periods—in most cases the growth periods would directly correspond to the times there were significant relationships with one or more people. This supports a study made to pinpoint the difference between happy and unhappy people. It concluded that the single most impressive difference between the two groups was that happy people were successfully involved with others, while unhappy people were not![1]

Healthy relationships are the primary ingredient for a good self-image. Many studies have shown that self-image is not related to family wealth, social class, father's occupation, education, geographical living area, or always having a mother at home. It comes from the quality of the relationships that exist between a person and those who play a significant role in his life, especially while he's growing up. Whenever someone says, "I'm inadequate," he is not only commenting on his self-image, but also on the quality of his relationships from which he has constructed his self-image.[2]

Fighting the Second Law of Thermodynamics

Cultivating love relationships is absolutely necessary for your mental health, but there's a basic problem which constantly works against it!

> *Mental Maxim #13*
> Left to themselves—things tend to go from bad to worse!

Unfortunately relationships are no exception! The second physical law of thermodynamics states that everything is disintegrating, and that's also true in relationships. Contrary to popular opinion, relationships do not work out by themselves! If they're left to themselves they disintegrate! Communication tends to break down when it isn't cultivated, and that produces repressed thoughts and feelings. It usually doesn't take long before the repression builds up and anger and resentment and a pressure-cooker life style results. If the lid on the pressure were ever opened, the repressed ugliness would seep out. Therefore, the pressure-cooker life style relates primarily on a surface level. In order for you to cultivate love relationships, you must break the barrier (and habit) of surface relationships! You must fight against the second law of thermodynamics in relationships!

Mental Maxim #14
Love your neighbor as yourself. If you don't love yourself, your neighbor's in a heap of trouble!

There are three primary relationships in which love must be cultivated: *inner* (yourself), *intimate* (family and friends), and *infectious* (everyone else). And each of them must be cultivated in their respective order to produce a healthy context of relationships.

LOVE: INNER RELATIONSHIPS

Self-Love Is Not Selfishness

Before even considering how to cultivate love relationships with other people, you must cultivate a love relationship with *you!* *Self-love* is not to be confused with *selfishness!* In his book, *Escape from Freedom,* Erich Fromm distinguishes between the two: "Selfishness is not identical with self-love but its very opposite. Selfishness is one kind of greediness. Like all greediness, it contains an insatiability, as a consequence of which there is never any real satisfaction. Greed is a bottomless pit which exhausts the person in an endless effort to satisfy the need without ever reaching satisfaction. . . . the selfish person is always anxiously concerned with himself; he is never satisfied, is always restless, always driven by the fear of not getting enough, of missing something, of being deprived of something. He is filled with burning envy of anyone who might have more. . . . this type of person is basically not fond of himself at all, but deeply dislikes himself. . . . Selfishness is rooted in this very lack of fondness for oneself. . . . narcissism, like selfishness, is an overcompensation for the basic lack of self-love. . . . He loves neither others nor himself."[3] Self-love is not only good, but absolutely necessary in expressing love for others!

Self-knowledge Prevents the Cover-Up

To love yourself, you must know yourself! Your make-up is basically physical and psychological. Physically (physiologically not cosmetically), your make-up is the same as every other human being on earth. Self-knowledge of the human, physical make-up assists you in loving your body properly. You know your need to eat, sleep, and exercise properly. (*Or do you?*) Psychological self-knowledge is not as easy! Your psychological make-up is varied and hidden. However, each person does have a combination of strengths and weaknesses.

Mental Maxim #15
The truly strong person knows and is able to express both his strengths and his weaknesses.

You weaken your personness by focusing on one or the other. Too many people are practicing *psychological cover-up*—either focusing on the weaknesses and covering up the strengths or focusing on the strengths and covering up the weaknesses. In either case, whether it's conscious or subconscious, the cover-up comes from a lack of self-knowledge. *It's difficult to love someone you don't know!* And as you attempt to relate to others, and are continually hiding the real *you*, the cover-up can become exhausting! Of course, you also always run the risk of not being able to cover-up all the time!

Mental Maxim #16
You can fool all the people some of the time and some of the people all of the time, but you can't fool MOM!

Self-Deception Will Trap You

Self-deception is the greatest denial of reality. Remember, *reality isn't the way you wish things to be, nor the way they appear to be, but the way they actually are!* Self-deception occurs when you allow your mind to be anesthetized to the point that your thoughts about you and life are not the way they actually are, but only the way you wish them to be! Later, when you come out of the "ether," you are filled with disappointment, anger, bitterness, and resentment toward everyone and everything that was a part of your particular deception. In most every situation involving self-deception, you feel you were "shafted"! But in nearly every one of those situations, your reaction was misdirected! If you're going to get upset, get upset with the source of the deception—*you!*

The traps of self-deception are endless! A never-ending process of life is learning to strip away the deceptive and get down to reality—the truth! Let's take a quick look at a few of the more common self-deception traps.

THE EXPECTATION TRAP is when your expectations are filled with helium and are lifted up above reality.

Mental Maxim #17
When expectations exceed reality, disappointment is certain.

Get rid of the helium and get down to reality!

An offshoot of the EXPECTATION TRAP is the self-deception that other people care as much about what you're doing as you do. It's a nice thought, but it's just not true! It's a CARE TRAP!

Mental Maxim #18
No one cares as much about what you're doing as you do.

Others may care, and they may care a lot, but they will never care as much as you do. If you expect them to, then prepare yourself for frustration and disappointment!

Perhaps one of the most damaging self-deception traps is the THAT WILL BE IT TRAP. When we retire, *that will be it!* When we buy a new 450 SL Mercedes Benz, *that will be it!* When we completely remodel our house, *that will be it!* When I graduate and move into my own apartment, *that will be it!* Unfortunately, once you get to *it*, *it* disappears!

Mental Maxim #19
If your primary focus is on material things, you'll eventually lose it all.

In everything you do, strip away the deceptive and get down to reality—the truth. And not only should you strive for reality in everything you do, but also in everything you are! Then and only then will you be able to consistently love your self.

LOVE: INTIMATE RELATIONSHIPS

Once you begin cultivating love for yourself, you're freed to cultivate love relationships with other people, to love on the intimate level. This level includes your family and close friends.

Three Faces of Love

There are three types of lovers in the world—*takers, givers,* and *giver-takers!* The *takers* are conditional lovers. "I love you as long as you do thus and thus for me." In other words, "I love you, because you love me!" The taker is extremely insecure, and he doesn't really love himself. You can't give away something you don't possess and he has nothing to give to anyone else. Since the taker doesn't possess love, he seeks to possess people and manipulate them to get it. By definition, his action of possessing other people for love gratification can hardly be called a relationship. At the very most it's an unhealthy relationship. Therefore, this "love relationship" isn't a long-term context for healthy personness.

The *givers* are unconditional lovers. "I love you—no matter what you say, do or think!" It's a love of commitment for the benefit of another's good, rather than the taker's approach of loving for his own, selfish benefit. This is the best kind of love, but it does have a limitation. Consistently being a giver over the long term won't satisfy your personness. Imperfect man needs something in return.

The *giver-takers* are interdependent lovers. This kind of love says, "I love you unconditionally, and I need you to complete me!" The giver-takers love and complete one another. Most books about love on the market today reject this kind of love as being unhealthy. They reason that people shouldn't love interdependently because they'll lose too much of their self in the process. But in the interdependent love of the giver-takers only selfishness—not his self-love or personness—is lost.

Mental Maxim #20
When your selfishness dies in an intimate relationship, your personness finds new life.

A giver-taker relationship makes you more of a person. It enhances and completes your personness. It's a two-way relationship—a value-for-value relationship—and that makes it a very healthy context for the growth of *you*. A giver-taker love relationship accepts the other person and yet encourages him/her to the very best.

Giver-takers: Weird Women and Strange Men

Marriage is the most intimate love relationship possible. A *maximum marriage is where a man and woman cultivate an intimate oneness and through that oneness find themselves more fulfilled individually.*

If you're married and cultivating a love relationship with your mate, hopefully you're experiencing a maximum marriage. Of course, it does take being a student of your mate's needs and trying to meet them and studying your mate to find out what makes him/her *tick* or *ticked!*

More than anything else your mate needs to know and feel that you care. My wife came out of the back bedroom one day where a "nuclear" blast had just occurred and sat down next to me on the couch. After she told me about her problem in the back bedroom, I with all my insight, knowledge, wisdom, and vast counseling experience gave her the answer to her problem in the back bedroom. Then she turned on me! She didn't want an *answer* to her problem. All she wanted to know was, "Do you care? Do you care that a nuclear blast just took place in the back bedroom? If you *do*, then I'll go back and clean it up, but if you don't, then there's going to be another nuclear blast here in the living room—and when it's over you're going to need cleaning up!"

Women are weird and men are strange! Despite what many voices are saying today, men and women are different! For instance, women initially react in the "immediate" and men react "long-range." The wife seems to ask continually, "Do you love me? Are you sure you still love me?" After the husband has been bombarded by the same question for what seems to him an eternity, he responds, "I told you I loved you when we got married, and it's still in effect, until I tell you otherwise!" Men and women are different!

I came home one evening and announced to my wife, "Honey, we're going to the Middle East for a month!" She didn't seem very excited. She asked me four questions: "How can we afford it? What about the kids? What about the house? What about the car?" (She was reacting in the "immediate.") I was furious and frustrated! Here we had a chance of a lifetime before us, and she was asking "crazy" questions. But it was my fault. I should have realized where she was coming from, and phrased my announcement differently: "Honey, I have a topic sentence and a few things to follow. The topic sentence is we're going to the Middle East for a month! Hold it: It's paid for, I know who'll keep the kids, the house will probably stay right here, and the car will remain in the garage." Now I've met her need for the "immediate," and she's free to become excited about the trip. Women are weird!

But men are strange! Men initially react in the "long-range." When a wife sees her husband's body walk in the door in the evening, she makes a false assumption. She assumes he came home. This couldn't be further from the truth. He's still at work! He just sent his body on ahead, so it could be there on time for dinner! Normally I recommend that the wife tell her husband he's home. She might say something like, "Honey, it's so good to have you hoooommme!" If she can give him a few subtle clues, it helps him to catch up with his body quicker! Men are strange!

Giver-takers: Family and Friends

The most intimate relationship of marriage is the model for the other intimate relationships—family and friends. The two most important principles for all intimate relationships are *commitment* and *communication*.

Commitment is to the preservation of each person in the relationship while cultivating a oneness and completion together. It's a preservation of the "I love you and need you" relationship.

Communication is the expression of the giver-taker commitment. There must be interaction in your intimate love relationships. Through communication you build a reservoir of shared experiences together. Communication is to love what blood is to the body. When the flow of blood stops, the body dies, and when the exchange of communication stops, the love dies. There are no winners and losers in communication, only winners. Neither person is ever required to give up or to give in but only to give. In communication you can never end up with less than you were—only more. To live in commitment and communication with another is to live twice. Joys are doubled by exchange, and burdens are cut in half by sharing.[4]

Mental Maxim #21

Commitment is the glue which holds a love relationship together. Communication is the oil which gives a love relationship life.

LOVE: INFECTIOUS RELATIONSHIPS

The third level of love relationships are the infectious relationships. This level includes everyone else you encounter in your world. They're infectious, because you can either boost or bury these people during the brief moments you relate to them. It may be at the office, in the market, at the local department store, along the beach, in the booth across from you in a restaurant, or sitting in the car next to you at a red light!

These relationships are the briefest of all, yet they occur often and are not insignificant! When your eyes meet those of someone else, you relay a message. You reflect either personness or nonpersonness! You can change the complexion of a person's entire day through a brief relationship with him, yet even more incredible is that you can transform *your* whole day through the same brief relationship! *It's a close encounter of the briefest kind! But it's life-changing!*

Mental Maxim #22
What sunshine is to flowers, smiles are to people.

In giving yourself a mental you must:

First: *choose a realistic base*

Second: *cultivate love relationships:*
inner (yourself)
intimate (family and friends)
infectious (everyone else)
And finally . . . .

18

You're Responsible to Your World

STEP THREE: CREATE A RESPONSIBLE DESTINY

THERE'S A RESPONSIBILITY crisis going on in our world! No one seems to be responsible in anything, and an enormous amount of energy is exerted in thinking over who to blame. There's a little rhyme that says: "The person who can smile when things go wrong has thought of someone to blame it on!"

Two extremes exist in the responsibility crisis. The first is *irresponsibility.* This is when you're not responsible at all with respect to people or things. The other extreme is *over-responsibility.* This is when you feel responsible for everything and everyone. The deceiving thing about this last extreme is you are responsible *for* some things (not all, only some), but you are not responsible *for* other people! The problem with being responsible *for* other people (whether they be family or friends) is you inevitably relieve them from responsibility altogether. That's why some children are resistant, and maybe even shocked, when their parents expect responsibility from them. Since their parents have been responsible *for* them, and they should be, why do the children need to be concerned about responsibility! The catch is the parents should also be transferring responsibility to their children as they grow up.

Instead of being responsible *for* people in your relationships, try being responsible *to* them, *to* the development of their personness. That means being responsible *to* stimulate them toward a more realistic, relational and responsible life style.

Creativity in a Wind-up Society

Modern man easily becomes subject to technology and mass impersonalization. Rather than being free and creative and able to take advantage of a higher technology, he becomes less than a zero. The principle of success has become so important that anything which leads to it is considered morally right. But this twists man and denies his essential humanity. If you strive for success at the cost of being human, what have you gained? When the job is more important than the humanity of the worker, our society is sick. It's a wind-up society! [1]

In a Swedish automobile factory, there has been a reorganization of the way in which the cars are made. They used to be made on an assembly line, each man doing one task over and over again and never seeing the results of his labor. Now the factory is organized into groups of ten men who make a portion of a car from beginning to end and then start all over again and make another one. This is a more humane way of working. It gives a sense of creativity because the thing created is immediately seen as it takes shape under the hands of the worker. [2]

The fact is if there is no individual identity, then any job is totally unimportant. Any job becomes a threat to you if it stifles all search and swallows up your individuality, making you indistinguishable from any other cog in society's machine. In such a situation, the job refashions you, and all that's left for you is never to act but only to react. [3]

Only in creative activity do you externalize the unique identity you have as a person. What distinguishes you from the animal is the possibility of being creative beyond the immediate environment. You can alter and enlarge your environment, the porpoise can't. You can, also to some extent, change your future by your creative activity.[4]

You and only you are responsible *for* your self! And you are responsible *to* your world. The most responsible thing you can do *for* you and *to* your world is to express your personness through creative activity. It's only through this creativity (acting instead of reacting) that you are able to break out of the wind-up society and take control of your future. In giving yourself a mental, you must create a responsible destiny!

Mental Group—The Ultimate Bomb Shelter!

Two is company and three is a crowd, but four or more may be the best shelter against the debris from the time bombs! More than a strong will, a big heart, or a cheerful disposition, people may need close, supportive friends and families to ward off depression. Sociologists at the University of Florida report that "the availability of one's friends and kin has more to do with vulnerability to depression than the number and kind of stressful events one suffers. . . . People under the most stress who had close human contacts coped better with the stress than similar people without such supports."[5]

If supportive relationships are effective in sheltering people from the stress of the time bombs, then why not form a group—*mental group!* The mental group is for stimulation, support, and survival! And it can become a dynamic context for the process of giving yourself a mental!

The first purpose of the mental group is *stimulation.* The primary action in fulfilling this purpose is *to search for principles of life together.* This action will help defuse the philosophical time bomb.

There are numerous ways to carry out a search. You can read books, listen to tapes, pose questions, or discuss various resource materials. Each member might be responsible to the group for taking a turn in leading the search. An extremely crucial guideline for effective stimulation is each person must operate from a learner-stance (a commitment to think) rather than a debater-stance (a commitment to spout). The end result of stimulation is for each person to *choose a realistic base* for his personness.

The second purpose of the mental group is *support.* The primary action in fulfilling this purpose is *to share the good and the bad.* This action is necessary for defusing the sociological time bomb.

The mental group becomes an extended family unit. Because of our mobile society, people are separated from their natural family members. The supportive nature of the mental group can help fill this gap. You need someone you can share your joys and sorrows with. There's nothing that can boost your self-esteem more than to know somebody's on your team —someone who won't put you on a performance treadmill. The supportive mental group should provide a positive, affirming atmosphere where you can be yourself.

One of the greatest benefits of the mental group's support is that it will balance your perspective. I've gone to a mental group some evenings when I thought the world must have voted it "Dump on Tim" week. Yet, after hearing the life-struggles of others in the group, my perspective radically changed. I realized I wasn't the only one who was under a pile, and compared to the piles some were shoveling, the mountain I carried into the group turned into a molehill! The end result of support is for each person to *cultivate love relationships.*

The third purpose of the mental group is *survival.* The primary action in fulfilling this purpose is *to strategize the defusion of the remaining time bombs*—the physical (ecological-chemical-biological), the metaphysical (psychological-religious-parapsychological), and the regulators (educational-political). Because of the overpowering nature of these particular time bombs, you dare not act alone in attempting to defuse them. They're just too awesome, even after choosing a base and cultivating healthy relationships.

The mental group must become an action group in your community. Otherwise, it will fizzle out in no time. Two problems are common when a group attempts action. The first is the problem of "battles versus war." Groups tend to busy themselves so much with the winning of the battles that they lose the war! They take a short-term approach to strategizing—"patchwork planning." Instead each action must be a move toward winning the war—even if a few battles are lost!

The second is the problem of attempting perfect plans. Since perfection is hard to come by, procrastination usually settles in while you're trying to acquire it. Then, after only a short period of time, procrastination moves into paralysis!

Mental Maxim #24
A good plan today is better than a perfect plan tomorrow.

Through a strategy, you're out for survival! The end result of survival is for the mental to corporately, as well as individually, *create a responsible destiny.*

The underlying purpose of the mental group is to motivate you to think and when you are forced into the thinking process, your perspective on life is expanded! The mental group is an effective vehicle for compelling you to expand your perspective on life's 3 R's—*Reality, Relationship, and Responsibility!*

In giving yourself a mental you are to:
   (1) Choose a realistic base
   (2) Cultivate love relationships
   (3) Create a responsible destiny
But how can you continue the process?

When I work,
I works hard.
When I sit,
I sits loose.
And when I think
I falls asleep!

19

Overhaul Your Personness

Mental Maxim #25

You can commit yourself to something over and over again, but if you don't talk your mind into going along with it, your commitment will fizzle out.

Operating Power of the Mind

You can commit yourself to choose a realistic base, to cultivate love relationships, and to create a responsible destiny, but there's a built-in fizzle in your commitment unless your mind is constantly in control. Your mind is the control-center of everything that's *you!* It's "the brains of your outfit!"

In addition to being a control-center, your mind is also a giant tape recorder. It has efficiently recorded everything you've ever said, heard, seen, felt, and done! Through hypnotism a person can be taken back through his life all the way to childhood. If he's asked to write his name the way he did at 16, he'll write it just the way his mind recorded it when he was 16. When he's asked to write his name the way he did at 7, the hypnotized person will print it exactly the way his mind recorded it when he was 7. The operating power of the mind is truly phenomenal!

The mind has also been compared to a computer! What you put into a computer is what comes out and the same is true for your mind. If you store negative information in your mind, negatives must come out! Garbage in, garbage out! It's like the "sowing and reaping" principle. Once the seed thought (positive or negative) has been sown, the feelings and actions which are reaped from it will be the same as the seed.

The operating power of the mind can also affect physical ailments. There's an increasing amount of evidence being gathered to support the notion that people even choose things like tumors, influenza, arthritis, heart disease, "accidents" and many other infirmities—including cancer—which have always been considered things that just happen to people. In treating what have been labeled "terminally ill" patients, some researchers now believe that helping the patient not to want the disease, in any form, may be a means of ameliorating the internal killer. Some cultures treat pain in this way, taking complete power over the mind and making self-control synonymous with mind control.[2]

The mind, which is composed of ten billion, billion working parts, has enough storage capacity to accept ten new facts every second. It has been conservatively estimated that the human mind can store an amount of information equivalent to one hundred trillion words, and that all of us use but a tiny fraction of this storage space. What you carry around with you in your head is a powerful instrument![3]

If you are going to take control of your life, you must take control of your mind—the control-center! And it's up to you to take control of your own mind, and then start being, feeling, and behaving in the ways you choose!

Mental Maxim #26
As you think, you are.
As you think, you feel.
As you think, you behave.

208 □ *The Defusing of the Time Bombs*

Overall Prosperity of Meditation

If you want to control your mind then you must feed it selectively! Selective feeding of the mind is called meditation. The most popular form of meditation today is "emptying" your mind, but true meditation doesn't occur in a vacuum. True meditation involves feeding your mind!

I must confess that meditation is the most difficult activity I know of, yet I know of no other activity that is more life-changing! The results of meditation are endless! More valuable than anything else is that meditation will widen your perspective on your self, your relationships, and your future.

A few years ago, I became hooked on meditation, just shortly after I'd chosen the Bible as my base for personness and universals. I'd heard a man speak on the subject of meditation, and I decided to try it. There was one particular area of my personality that I really wanted to change, and that was my nasty habit of going berserk when anyone messed with my car! I knew the habit had to go or I'd soon be traveling the road alone for lack of friends!

I began meditating on a paragraph in the Bible where it says, "Consider it all joy, my brethren, when you encounter various trials; knowing that the testing of your faith produces endurance" (James 1: 2, 3).

As I moved into the process of overhauling my mind by meditating on this paragraph, some exciting things happened! I experienced an all-out war on my nice, new car! It seemed like every parking lot had a roving destroyer just waiting for me to leave my car so he could dent or scratch it! And around every corner was a car sledgehammer with my car's license number on it! Within three weeks after I started meditating, I experienced four major accidents! My car was demolished! I found myself suffering from *automobile paranoia.*

But in each of these "various trials" (from scratches to scrapes to smashes) something strange was happening to my normal reaction-style. At each occurrence, just when I was ready to move into "berserkness," a sign lit up in my mind's eye. It said, "consider it all joy . . . when you encounter various trials; knowing that the testing of your faith produces endurance!" When this appeared, I was reminded of the big picture (a wider perspective on life) and chose not to blow up. Needless to say, I was impressed with my new behavior, I was in control! By expanding your perspective on life, meditation gives your "control-center" more options to choose from when it's time for action! I prescribe meditation for those seeking counsel more than anything else! It shouldn't necessarily be used as the total cure for a problem, but it does serve an important part. As a *psychological tranquilizer* the effect of meditation calms you down and lets you think about your problem—which is expanding your perspective on life!

Meditation brings the most genuine prosperity you could ever possess. Peace of mind, wisdom, control of annoying habits, relief from destructive stress, the ability to view your problems through a wider perspective, a greater sensitivity to yourself and your relationships, patience and endurance during "various trials," hope for personal change and growth, and so on. Whatever *your* stress problem, you'll find meditation can be a mental adrenaline that will boost you into the "controls" of *you*, your relationships, and your future!

Overhauling Process of the Mental

The overhauling process is preparatory work for "psychological digestion." The "mental food" you order for meditation will determine the kinds of digestion you'll experience. If you order "junk food" for your mind, you may experience problems in your "psychological digestion"—like "psychological heartburn!"

Once you've chosen your base for right and wrong—your base for personness—you can use the universal principle of life taken from your base as a menu. I "order" from my base (the Bible), and I've found it most satisfying in my personness! In fact, I've found that the principles found in the Bible are so true to people as they are and life as it is that they can be used as a source of meditation by people who don't have a base yet. Many such people start with Psalms and Proverbs, which are especially applicable for a daily diet, and then later adopt the whole Bible as their base.

After ordering your "mental food," you must *bite* into it! A paragraph contains a basic unit of thought and seems to work best for a bite-sized chunk in the overhauling process. Next you must *chew* it. The chewing process is extremely important, as the more you think about your "mental food" the deeper it sinks into your psyche. I normally suggest chewing on a paragraph or principle for about a week. Writing out your "mental food" on a 3 by 5 card can be helpful in meditating. You can put it on your desk, fasten it to the refrigerator door or carry it with you so you can keep chewing on it throughout the week. Finally, you must *swallow* your "mental food." Swallowing is the process of applying the principles of life to your life-situations, of making wise choices which are in line with the principles.

No matter *how* you meditate, make the choice *to* meditate! Meditation is the overhauling process of the mental. Without it, the mental could easily become just another temporary hype and you're likely to contract the mind's most debilitating disease—*mental constipation.* That's when all thinking comes to a screeching halt!

Have You Ever Felt Like Humpty Dumpty?

Why not give yourself a mental checkup? It's the process of *choosing a realistic base, cultivating love relationships,* and *creating a responsible destiny.* It's the process of experiencing and expressing your personness.

A priest and a new convert were playing a round of golf. The new convert had a terrible temper, and after missing the putt on his first three holes he lost his temper! He yelled out, "I missed! How could I miss!" He kicked up a piece of the green, broke his putter over his knee, and threw the pieces as far as he could heave them. It was an incredible outburst of anger! The priest was shocked and he felt it his duty to warn the new convert of the possible consequences of such a terrible temper. So, the priest began to preach, "My friend, I feel impelled to warn you of what might happen to you someday after an angry reaction such as you just displayed. There is an angel called Zapriel whose one primary mission is to search for the worst outbursts of anger and zap the ones responsible! When Zapriel finds such an outburst the clouds part, a fireball forms in the sky and it strikes and burns the body of the one responsible! I'm telling you this, my friend, because you are a likely candidate for zapping. I've never seen such an outburst over something so insignificant as a missed putt! I'm warning you, if you don't turn from your wicked ways, you're going to burn!"

The new convert listened carefully to the admonition of the priest, and he had every intention of heeding it. Then at the ninth hole, the new convert tore out a huge divot (a hunk of dirt) with his driver and missed the ball completely! You'd think he hadn't heard a word the priest had said. "I missed! How could I miss!", he yelled out at the top of his lungs. He kicked up a piece of the fairway, broke his driver over his knee, and threw the pieces as far as he could heave them.

All of a sudden the clouds parted, a fireball formed in the sky, and it struck the priest and burned him to a crisp!

An awesome silence filled the golf course. All that could be heard was a voice echoing in the heavens, "I missed! How could I miss!"

Like Zapriel, you have one primary mission. Yours is to fully experience and express your personness—you were created to be—*you!* Wouldn't it be a shame to miss?

Chapter 1.
1. "How Many People?" (New York: Foreign Policy Association, No. 218, December, 1973), p. 4.
2. "How to Defuse the Population Bomb," *Time* (October 24, 1977).
3. Dr. Paul R. Ehrlich, *The Population Bomb* (Ballatine Books, Inc., 1968), p. 13.
4. Op. cit., *Time.*
5. "Population and the Sierra Club" (San Francisco, California: III, 3000, June, 1975), p. 4.
6. Ehrlich, *Population Bomb*, pp. 25, 26.
7. Ibid., pp. 18–19.
8. Ibid., p. 34.
9. Op. cit., "How Many People?," p. 65.
10. Ibid., p. 57.
11. Op. cit., "Population and the Sierra Club," p. 3.
12. "Worldwatch Paper 5: Twenty-two Dimensions of the Population Problem," (Washington D.C.: Worldwatch Institute, 1976), p. 67.
13. Op. cit., "Population and the Sierra Club," p. 3.
14. "Population" (Washington D.C.: Population Crisis Committee, April, 1976), p. 1.
15. Op. cit., "Worldwatch," p. 49.
16. Ibid., p. 50.
17. Op. cit., "Population," p. 3.
18. Ehrlich, *Population Bomb*, p. 28.
19. Population Reference Bureau (Washington, D.C.: Selection No. 34, November, 1970), p. 4.
20. Ehrlich, *Population Bomb*, p. 149.
21. *Ibid.*, p. 156.
22. Op. cit., "Population and the Sierra Club," p. 4.
23. Op. cit., "How Many People?," p. 33.
24. Op. cit., "Worldwatch," p. 65.
25. Ibid., p. 11.
26. Ibid., p. 58.
27. Ibid., p. 59.
28. Ibid., p. 74.
29. Ehrlich, *Population Bomb*, p. 133.
30. Op. cit., "Worldwatch," pp. 32–34.
31. Ibid., p. 34.
32. Ibid., p. 51.
33. Ibid., p. 61.
34. Ibid., p. 15.
35. Ibid., p. 52.
36. Ehrlich, *Population Bomb*, p. 62.
37. Op. cit., "Worldwatch," p. 19.
38. Ibid., p. 19.
39. Ibid., pp. 26, 27.
40. Ibid., p. 25.
41. Ehrlich, *Population Bomb*, p. 97.

42. Op. cit., "Worldwatch," pp. 35, 36.
43. Ehrlich, *Population Bomb,* p. 61.
44. Op. cit., "Worldwatch," p. 26.
45. Ibid., pp. 19, 20.
46. Ehrlich, *Population Bomb,* p. 128.
47. Op. cit., "Worldwatch," p. 43.
48. Ibid., p. 44.
49. Ibid., p. 44.
50. Ehrlich, *Population Bomb,* p. 130.

Chapter 2.
1. "Environmental Contaminants in Foods" (New York: New York State Agricultural Exchange Station, Special Report No. 9, November, 1972), p. 1.
2. Ibid., p. 2.
3. Ibid., p. 1.
4. "Food Additives: What They Are—How They Are Used" (Washington D.C.: Manufacturing Chemists' Assn., 1974), p. 15.
5. "Food Additives: Who Needs Them?" (Washington, D.C.: Manufacturing Chemists' Assn., 1974), p. 3.
6. Ibid., p. 6.
7. Op. cit., "Food Additives: What They Are—How They Are Used," pp. 16, 17.
8. Ibid., p. 19.
9. Ibid., pp. 22, 23.
10. Ibid., p. 38.
11. Ibid., pp. 39, 40.
12. "FDA Bans Saccharin, Says It Causes Cancer in Animals," *L.A. Times,* March 10, 1977.
13. "The Ban on Saccharin: How? Why?," *L.A. Times,* March 20, 1977.
14. Op. cit., "FDA"
15. "Let's Stop Dumping U.S. Jobs" (Dow Chemical USA Commonwealth Club of California, January 27, 1978).
16. "Pesticides" (New York: A Scientists' Institute for Public Information Workbook, 1970), p. 10.
17. "Understanding Pesticides" (Washington, D.C.: National Agricultural Chemicals Assn., 1972), pp. 10, 11.
18. Ibid., p. 11.
19. "Pesticides and Your Environment" (Washington D.C.: National Wildlife Federation, 1972), p. 3.
20. Op. cit., "Pesticides," p. 14.
21. Op. cit., "Pesticides and Your Environment," p. 4.
22. Op. cit., "Pesticides," p. 15.
23. Op. cit., "Pesticides and Your Environment," pp. 3, 4.
24. Op. cit., "Pesticides," p. 15.
25. William Tucker, "Of Mites and Men," *Harper's Magazine,* August, 1978.

26. G. W. Pearson, "Politics and the Engineer" (Dow Chemical U.S.A., Organic Chemicals Department, March, 1978).
27. Op. cit., "Pesticides," p. 3.
28. Marvin Zeldin, "The Campaign for Cleaner Air" (New York: Public Affairs Pamphlet No. 494, 1973), p. 3.
29. Ibid., p. 13.
30. Ibid., p. 15.
31. Ibid., p. 16.
32. Gladwin Hill, "Cleansing Our Waters" (New York: Public Affairs Pamphlet No. 497, 1973), p. 2.
33. Ibid., pp. 5, 6.
34. Ibid., p. 3.
35. "Air Pollution" (New York: A Scientists' Institute for Public Information Workbook, 1970), p. 3.

Chapter 3.
1. Francis Schaeffer, *Back to Freedom and Dignity* (Downers Grove, Ill.: Inter-Varsity Press, 1972), p. 1.
2. Gordon Rattray Taylor, *The Biological Time Bomb* (Cleveland, Ohio: The World Publishing Co., 1968), jacket cover.
3. Robert L. Sinsheimer, "Genetic Engineering: The Modification of Man" (Report to the Subcommittee on Science, Research, and Development of the Committee on Science and Astronautics, U.S. House of Representatives, 92nd Congress, November, 1972), p. 63.
4. Taylor, *Biological Time Bomb*, p. 46.
5. Leon R. Kass, "Babies by Means of In Vitro Fertilization: Unethical Experiments on the Unborn?" (The New England Journal of Medicine, vol. 285, November, 1971), pp. 104, 105.
6. Joseph Fletcher, "Ethical Aspects of Genetic Controls" (The New England Journal of Medicine, vol. 285, September 30, 1971), p. 70.
7. Schaeffer, *Back to Freedom and Dignity*, p. 21.
8. Taylor, *Biological Time Bomb*, pp. 112, 113.
9. Ibid., pp. 102, 103.
10. Ibid., p. 108.
11. "Genetic Engineering: Evolution of a Technological Issue" (Report to the Subcommittee on Science, Research, and Development of the Committee on Science and Astronautics, U.S. House of Representatives, 92nd Congress, November, 1972), p. 2.
12. Ibid., pp. 2, 3.
13. Op. cit., Leon R. Kass, pp. 103, 104.
14. Ibid., p. 102.
15. Op. cit., Joseph Fletcher, pp. 74, 75.
16. Theodore Friedmann and Richard Roblin, "Gene Therapy for Genetic Disease?" (Science, vol. 175, March 3, 1972), p. 86.
17. Op. cit., "Genetic Engineering," pp. 4–6.
18. "Prospects for Designed Genetic Change" (A Transcript Report from the National Advisory General Medical Sciences Council of

the National Institute of General Medical Sciences, National Institutes of Health, Bethesda, Maryland, March 20, 1970), p. 24.
19. Op. cit., "Genetic Engineering," p. 23.
20. Ibid., p. 26.
21. "Doctors Isolate Gene, Say They Can Spot Defects," *L.A. Times,* July 27, 1978.
22. Op. cit., "Genetic Engineering," p. 14.
23. Ibid., p. 15.
24. Op. cit., Joseph Fletcher, pp. 69, 70.
25. "World's First 'Test Tube Baby' to Be Born Soon," *L.A. Times,* July 12, 1978.
26. Schaeffer, *Back to Freedom and Dignity,* p. 25.
27. Op. cit., "Genetic Engineering," p. 21.
28. Ibid., p. 30.
29. Op. cit., Joseph Fletcher, p. 66.

Chapter 4.
1. Robert A. Harper, *Psychoanalysis and Psychotherapy* (New York: A Spectrum Book—Prentice Hall, Inc., 1959), pp. 11, 12.
2. Ibid., pp. 13, 14.
3. Ibid., p. 20.
4. Ibid., p. 45.
5. Ibid., p. 59.
6. Ibid., p. 49.
7. Viktor E. Frankl, *Man's Search for Meaning* (New York: Pocket Books, 1959), p. 176.
8. Ibid., pp. 82, 83.
9. William Glasser, *Reality Therapy* (New York: Harper & Row Publications, 1965), p. xii.
10. Ibid., p. 122.
11. "Skinner's Utopia: Panacea, or Path to Hell?," *Time,* September 20, 1971, p. 47.
12. Ibid.
13. Ibid.
14. "TM; Penetrating the Veil of Deception" (Berkeley, California: Christian World Liberation Front pamphlet).
15. Maharishi Mahesh Yogi, *Transcendental Meditation* (New York: Signet Books 1963), jacket cover.
16. Op. cit., "TM"
17. Ibid.
18. Robert M. Goldenson, *The Encyclopedia of Human Behavior: Psychology, Psychiatry, and Mental Health* (New York: Doubleday & Company, Vol. 2, 1970), pp. 1330, 1331.
19. Ibid.
20. Adelaide Bry, *est* (New York: Avon Publishers, 1976), p. 31.
21. Ibid., p. 202.

Chapter 5.
1. Wm. J. Petersen, *Those Curious New Cults* (New Canaan, Connecticut: Keats Publishing, Inc., 1975), p. 205.
2. "The Cults—From Benign to Bizarre," *L.A. Times,* December 1, 1978.
3. "Scientology—Religion or Rip-off?," *Time,* April 5, 1976, p. 10.
4. "What Is This Church of Scientology?," *St. Petersburg Times,* March 14, 1976.
5. "Australia Probed Heart of Scientology," *St. Petersburg Times,* March 19, 1976.
6. *Daily Breeze,* Torrance, California, April 17, 1976.
7. "The Way, The Truth and Getting Out," *Philadelphia Daily News,* April 18, 1977.
8. Ibid.
9. Ibid.
10. J. Isamu Yamamoto, *Hare Krishna, Hare Krishna* (Downers Grove, Ill.: Inter-Varsity Press, 1978), p. 17.
11. Ibid.
12. Petersen, *Those Curious New Cults,* p. 149.
13. Huston Smith, *The Religions of Man* (New York: Mentor Books, 1958), p. 134.
14. *Those Curious New Cults,* p. 151.
15. Ibid., pp. 152, 153.
16. "Who Are the Children of God?" (Heerde, Holland: False Prophets Project, 1976), p. 1.
17. "The Children of God: Disciples of Deception," *Christianity Today,* February 18, 1977, p. 18.
18. "Tracking the Children of God," *Time,* August 22, 1977.
19. "Mad About Moon," *Time,* November 10, 1975.
20. Ibid.

Chapter 6.
1. Louisa E. Rhine, *PSI, What Is It?* (New York: Harper & Row Publishers, 1975, pp. 2, 3.
2. Ibid., p. 4.
3. Ibid., pp. 11, 12.
4. Ibid., p. 59.
5. Ibid., pp. 137, 138.
6. R. A. McConnell, "ESP and Credibility in Science" (University of Pittsburgh, Vol. 24, No. 5, May, 1969), p. 532.
7. Rhine, *PSI,* p. 48.
8. Ibid., p. 27.
9. Charles Richet, *Our Sixth Sense* (London: Rider & Co., 1920), pp. 67–92.
10. Rhine, *PSI,* pp. 40, 41.
11. Ibid., p. 51.
12. Ibid., p. 188.
13. Ibid., pp. 107, 108.

14. Ibid., pp. 109–114.
15. Op. cit., R. A. McConnell, p. 531.
16. Rhine, *PSI*, p. 187.
17. William J. Petersen, *Those Curious New Cults* (New Canaan, Conn.: Keats Publishing, Inc., 1973), pp. 17, 18.
18. Ibid., p. 15.
19. Ibid., p. 13.
20. Ibid., p. 23.
21. Walter R. Martin, *The Kingdom of the Cults* (Minneapolis, Minn.: Bethany Fellowship, Inc., 1965), p. 199.
22. Petersen, *Those Curious New Cults*, pp. 49, 50.
23. Ibid., pp. 60, 61.
24. Ibid., p. 66.
25. Ibid., p. 67.
26. Ibid., p. 62.
27. Ibid., pp. 64, 65.

Chapter 7.
1. "How to Get Quality Back into Schools," *U.S. News and World Report* (September 12, 1977), p. 31.
2. "Public Schools: They're Destroying Our Children," *American Opinion* (Belmont, Massachusetts: February, 1972), p. 1.
3. "City Schools in Crisis," *Newsweek* (September 12, 1977), p. 62.
4. Ibid., p. 63.
5. Ibid., p. 64.
6. Ibid.
7. Ibid.
8. *American Opinion*, op. cit., p. 1.
9. "Why Teachers Are Under Fire," *U.S. News and World Report* (December 12, 1977), p. 50.
10. Ibid.
11. Ibid.
12. "How to Get Quality into Schools," *U.S. News and World Report* (December 12, 1977) p. 32.
13. Ibid., p. 34.
14. "Why Teachers Are Under Fire," op. cit., p. 50.
15. "Back-to-School Blues," *Time* (September 18, 1978), p. 75.
16. Max Rafferty, *Suffer Little Children* (New York: A Signet Book, 1962), pp. 38, 39.
17. Ibid., pp. 82, 83.
18. Opal Moore, *Why Johnny Can't Learn* (Milford, Mich.: Mott Media, 1975), p. 48.
19. Rev. Edmund A. Opitz, from Introduction to *Intellectual Schizophrenia: Culture, Crisis and Education*, by Rousas J. Rushdoony; International Library, Philosophical and Historical Studies (Philadelphia, Penn.: Presbyterian and Reformed Publishing Co., 1971), pp. xx, xxi.

20. B. F. Skinner, *Walden Two* (London: The Macmillan Co., 1969), p. 264.
21. Op. cit., *Why Johnny Can't Learn*, p. 36.
22. Harold G. and June Grant Shane, "Forecast For The 70's," *Today's Education—NEA Journal*, January, 1969, pp. 31, 32.
23. Moore, *Why Johnny Can't Learn*, p. 41.
24. Alan Stang, "The N.E.A.—Dictatorship of the Educariat" (Belmont, Mass.: American Opinion, March, 1972), p. 6.
25. Peter H. Wagschal, "Illiterates with Doctorates: The Future of Education in an Electronic Age," *The Futurist*, August, 1978, p. 243.
26. Ibid., p. 244.
27. Philip Kitler, "Education Packagers: A Modest Proposal," *The Futurist*, August, 1978, p. 240.
28. "America's Press, Too Much Power for Too Few?" *U.S. News and World Report*, August 15, 1977, p. 31.
29. Ibid.
30. Ibid.
31. *TV Basics 19*, The Television Bureau of Advertising's Report on the Scope and Dimension of Television Today, Television Bureau of Advertising Inc., New York.
32. "TV's New Pitch," *U.S. News and World Report*, September 12, 1977, p. 23.

Chapter 8.
1. Rus Walton, *One Nation Under God* (Washington, D.C.: Third Century Publishers, 1975), pp. 231, 232.
2. Ibid., p. 233.
3. "Taxpayer's Liability Index" (Washington, D.C.: National Taxpayer's Union, 325 Pennsylvania Ave., S.E., 20003).
4. "U.S. Goes Deeper and Deeper in the Hole," *U.S. News and World Report*, October 10, 1977, pp. 46, 47.
5. Walton, *One Nation Under God*, p. 201.
6. Op. cit., "Taxpayer's Liability Index."
7. Ibid.
8. Op. cit., *One Nation Under God*, pp. 182, 183.
9. Statistical Abstract of the United States, 1974, p. 265.
10. Ibid., p. 298.
11. Walton, *One Nation Under God*, p. 184.
12. Ibid., p. 186.
13. "Biggest Jobs Program in Decades—Is It a Boon or a Boondoggle?", *U.S. News & World Report*, May 23, 1977, p. 96.
14. Ibid.
15. Ibid., p. 98.
16. "Social Security Overhaul: "Who'll Pay the Bill," *U.S. News and World Report*, May 23, 1977, p. 91.
17. Ibid.
18. Ibid.

19. Ibid.
20. Ibid.
21. "Are Government Workers Overpaid?," *U.S. News and World Report*, September 12, 1977, pp. 34, 35.
22. Ibid.
23. Charles H. Smith, Jr. "The Furure Price of Neglect," *Vital Speeches of the Day*, October, 1974.
24. Walton, *One Nation Under God*, p. 154.
25. Ibid., pp. 164, 165.

Chapter 9.
1. Daniel Bell, *The Coming of Post-Industrial Society* (New York: Basic Books/Harper Colophon Books, 1973), pp. 313, 314.
2. Ibid., p. 314.
3. Ibid., p. 316.
4. Ibid., p. 314.
5. "As Crime in the U.S. Starts to Level Off -," *U.S. News and World Report*, October 10, 1977, pp. 89, 90.
6. Ibid., p. 90.
7. "The Youth Crime Plague," *Time*, July 11, 1977, p. 18.
8. Ibid., p. 25.
9. Ibid.
10. Ibid.
11. "The American Underclass," *Time*, August 29, 1977, pp. 14–16.
12. Ibid.
13. Ibid.
14. Ibid.
15. Walter Miller, "The Rumble This Time," *Psychology Today*, May, 1977, pp. 60, 61.
16. Ibid., pp. 60, 61.
17. Ibid., p. 58.
18. "The Mafia: Big, Bad and Booming," *Time*, May 16, 1977, p. 33.
19. Ibid.
20. Ibid., p. 35.
21. Ibid., p. 33.
22. "The Boon of Leisure—Where Americans Spend 160 Billions," *U.S. News and World Report*, May 23, 1977, p. 62.
23. "A Relentless Search for Fun and Fitness," *U.S. News and World Report*, May, 1978, p. 51.
24. Daniel Yankelovich, "The New Psychological Contracts," *Psychology Today*, May, 1978, p. 50.
25. "Role of Young Adults in the Years Ahead," *U.S. News and World Report*, May 27, 1978, p. 61.
26. Ibid., p. 62.
27. Ibid.
28. Ibid.

Chapter 10.
1. Karl Menninger, *Whatever Became of Sin?* (New York: Hawthorne Books, 1973), p. 9.
2. Ibid.
3. Ibid., pp. 10, 11.
4. Daniel Bell, *The Coming of Post-Industrial Society* (New York: Basic Books/Harper Colophon Books, 1973), p. 480.
5. J.N.D. Anderson, *Morality, Law and Grace* (Downers Grove, Ill.: Inter-Varsity Press, 1972), p. 39.
6. "Genetic Engineering: Evolution of a Technological Issue," Report to the Subcommittee on Science, Research, and Development of the Committee on Science and Astronautics, U.S. House of Representatives, 92nd Congress, November, 1972, p. 39.
7. Joseph Fletcher, "Ethical Aspects of Genetic Engineering Controls," The New England Journal of Medicine, Vol. 285, September 30, 1971, p. 65.
8. George G. Berg, "Water Pollution" (New York: A Scientists' Institute for Public Information Workbook, 1970), p. 5.
9. Op. cit., Joseph Fletcher, p. 75.
10. Ibid., p. 73.
11. Francis A. Schaeffer, *How Should We Then Live?* (Old Tappan, New Jersey: Fleming H. Revell Company, 1976), pp. 223, 224.
12. Ibid., pp. 224, 225.

Chapter 11.
1. Kenneth R. Pelletier, "Mind As Healer, Mind As Slayer," *Psychology Today*, February, 1977, p. 35.
2. Ibid.
3. Ibid.
4. Cecil Osborne, *Release from Fear and Anxiety* (Waco, Texas: Word Books, 1976), p. 15.
5. Ibid.
6. Ibid., p. 16.
7. Op. cit., *Psychology Today*, p. 82.
8. Ibid., p. 83.

Chapter 12.
1. Paul Goodman, *Growing Up Absurd* (New York: Random House, 1960), pp. 159, 169.
2. Kenneth R. Pelletier, "Mind As Healer, Mind As Slayer," *Psychology Today*, February, 1977, p. 82.
3. Earl Jabay, *The Kingdom of Self* (Plainfield, New Jersey: Logos International, 1974), p. 35.
4. Norman Wright, *The Christian Use of Emotional Power* (Old Tappan, New Jersey: Fleming H. Revell Company, 1974), p. 121.
5. *Long Beach Independent Press-Telegram*, January 24, 1973, pp. 121, 122.
6. Francis A. Schaeffer, *How Should We Then Live?* (Old Tappan, New Jersey: Fleming H. Revell Company, 1976), p. 205

7. Jabay, *The Kingdom of Self*, p. 48.
8. Bill Counts and Bruce Narramore, *Guilt and Freedom* (Santa Ana, California: Vision House Publishers, 1974), p. 8.
9. Ibid., pp. 8, 9.
10. Thomas A. Harris, *I'm O.K.—You're O.K.* (New York: Harper & Row Publishers, 1967), pp. 218, 219.
11. Ibid., p. 220.
12. Karl Menninger, *Whatever Became of Sin?* (New York: Hawthorne Books, 1973), pp. 4, 5.
13. Alvin Toffler, *Future Shock* (New York: Random House, 1970), pp. 4, 285.

Chapter 13.
1. John Powell, *Why Am I Afraid to Love?* (Niles, Ill.: Argus Communications Company, 1967), pp. 23, 24.
2. Alvin Toffler, *Future Shock* (New York: Random House, 1970), p. 238.
3. Ibid., p. 258.
4. Cecil Osborne, *Release from Fear and Anxiety* (Waco, Texas: Word Books, 1976), pp. 49, 50.
5. "Saving the Family," *Newsweek*, May 15, 1978, pp. 67, 68.
6. "The Battered Wife: What's Being Done?," *L.A. Times*, April 27, 1978.
7. Otto Kernberg, "Why Some People Can't Love," *Psychology Today*, June, 1978, p. 55.
8. Ibid., p. 56.
9. Ibid., pp. 56, 57.
10. Ibid., p. 58.
11. "Why It's Called the 'Me' Generation," *U.S. News and World Report*, March 27, 1978, p. 43.
12. Op. cit., *Newsweek*, p. 64.

Chapter 14.
1. Os Guinness, *Dust of Death* (Downers Grove, Ill.: Inter-Varsity Press, 1973), pp. 62, 63.
2. Charles Martin, *How Human Can You Get?* (Downers Grove, Ill.: Inter-Varsity Press, 1973), pp. 16, 17.
3. Ibid., p. 18.
4. David Myers, *The Human Puzzle* (New York: Harper & Row, 1978), p. 13.
5. "Just a Game of Chance?," *Newsweek*, April 26, 1971, p. 99.
6. Bertrand Russell, *A Free Man's Worship* (Portland, Maine: Thomas Mosher, 1927), p. 6.
7. "Skinner's Utopia: Panacea or Path to Hell?" *Time*, September 20, 1971.
8. Francis A. Schaeffer, *Back to Freedom and Dignity* (Downers Grove, Ill.: Inter-Varsity Press, 1972), p. 33.
9. Ibid., pp. 34, 35.

10. Martin, *How Human Can You Get?*, pp. 29, 30.
11. Schaeffer, *Back to Freedom and Dignity*, pp. 19, 20.
12. Ibid., p. 18.
13. Ibid., pp. 144, 145.
14. Myers, *The Human Puzzle*, p. 10.
15. Guinness, *Dust of Death*, p. 148.

Chapter 15.
1. Robert Ringer, *Looking Out for #1* (New York: Funk and Wagnalls, 1977), pp. 28, 29.
2. Ayn Rand, *The Virtue of Selfishness* (New York: The New American Library, Inc., Signet Books, 1964), p. 29.
3. Ringer, *Looking Out for #1*, p. 25.
4. Ibid.

Chapter 16.
1. Francis A. Schaeffer, *He Is There and He Is Not Silent* (Wheaton, Ill.: Tyndale House, 1972), p. 7.
2. Ibid., p. 8.
3. Ibid., pp. 8, 9.
4. Clark Pinnock, *Set Forth Your Case* (Chicago: Moody Press, 1967), pp. 33, 34.

Chapter 17.
1. Dorothy Corkille Briggs, *Your Child's Self-Esteem* (New York: Doubleday Publishers, 1970), p. 26.
2. Ibid., pp. 5, 19.
3. John Powell, *The Secret of Staying in Love* (Niles, Ill.: Argus Communications, 1974), p. 15.
4. Ibid., p. 188.

Chapter 18.
1. Udo Middelmann, *Pro-Existence* (Downers Grove, Ill.: Inter-Varsity Press, 1974), p. 27.
2. Ibid.
3. Ibid., p. 14.
4. Ibid., pp. 18, 19.
5. Christopher T. Cory, "Depressed? Try Friends," *Psychology Today*, October, 1978, p. 19.

Chapter 19.
1. Norman Wright, *The Christian Use of Emotional Power* (Old Tappan, New Jersey: Fleming H. Revell Company, 1974), pp. 24–26.
2. Wayne Dyer, *Your Erroneous Zones* (New York: Funk and Wagnalls, 1976), pp. 19, 20.
3. Ibid., p. 20.

Appendix

The Supernatural Factor

IN SEARCHING FOR A REALISTIC BASE for life I have discovered the Bible is more than adequate as a base and contains a supernatural factor as well. The following are a few reasons why I chose the Bible as my base:

Agnosticism . . . mysticism . . . atheism . . . pantheism . . . humanism . . . Zen Buddhism . . . existentialism. . . . As the labels of life continue to flow ad nauseum, people are swinging from one side of the pendulum to the other. The result is that many are suffering from "ism-itis." "Ism-itis" is a sort of motion sickness caused from swinging on the pendulum or watching others swing. Because of the resulting dizziness, very few people have stopped long enough to consider the overwhelming evidence that the personal God of the universe has revealed himself by written (Bible) and human (Jesus of Nazareth) means and desires a relationship with people.

I'm not talking about religion. Religion destroys people. Jesus told the religious leaders of His day that they were "snakes" and "painted tombstones." He was down on religion, and so am I. When I wanted to obtain my "ticket to heaven," I was told by religion that there were fifteen things I couldn't do. As I looked over the list, I was immediately depressed. Those were my goals in life! Then I was told there were four things I could and must do: 1) go to church on Sunday morning, 2) go to church on Sunday evening, 3) go to church on Wednesday evening, and 4) pray be-

This appendix is an excerpt from my book, *The Ultimate Lifestyle*, published by Vision House Publishers, 1977, Santa Ana, California 92705. Used by permission.

fore every meal. It all spelled out a four letter word to me—
BORE! Then I ran into a group that said all I had to do to get
my ticket was to let them dunk me in their tank. (This comes in
various forms: sprinkling, squirting, drowning, dry-cleaning, and
so on.) The only thing I gained from that experience was a wet
body. No, I'm not talking about religion. Because it blindly accepts a certain system of do's and don'ts and ignores more basic
issues, religion makes life miserable. It is comparable to a seda-
tive given to a dying person. It may make them feel better, but
they are still dying.

The supernatural factor is also not a blind or mystical leap in
the dark whereby one hopes to find meaning to life. It's based on
evidence and logic. It's not a nebulous, evasive or untouchable
factor. It's a body of solid facts upon which we can hang our faith,
clearly laid out so that we can know and understand them.

If you are willing to acknowledge the available evidence, examine it honestly, and make a reasoned evaluation, we can begin
to think through the supernatural factor. I challenge you to face
these facts openly.

THE SUPERNATURAL REVELATION

The first piece of evidence I would like to consider is whether
the Bible, comprised of the Old Testament and the New Testament, is a revelation from God. In order for you to think this
through, I'd like to offer you just a few reasons why I believe it is.

Unity

The first reason I believe the Bible is a supernatural revelation
from God is that it has incredible unity. It was written over a period of fifteen hundred years, by forty different writers, in three
different languages, and on three different continents. A lot of
people think that some group back in Jerusalem got together—the
First Bapterian Church or the Episcolics—and decided to write a
bunch of books. Then year after year they submitted them to the
University of Jerusalem, who at last one day put them to press and
called them the Bible. That's not true. It was written over many
centuries, and yet with unbelievable unity. You can read modern
books on different subjects, even from one university, from one
school of thought, and you will find vast differences. There may be
people working on the same committee, trying to come up with
some sort of book, and they'll disagree even on what chapters
should be included. So when you find a book written over a long
period of time, in a number of languages, by people with wide
cultural differences, and still see unity—you have something you
had better look into.

You will see the Old Testament, bursting and screaming out that
there is a Messiah coming, a Messiah who is needed because we
are wicked people who need to have our sin paid for. He's coming
—he's coming. You will see the New Testament, revealing a Mes-

siah who has come to pay for our sin. He's come—he's come. You see the tying of the two together, and it's absolutely beautiful. The unity.

Accuracy

The second reason why I believe that the Bible is a revelation from God is its accuracy. I divide this subject into two parts: the archaeological accuracy and the historical accuracy. I'm just going to give you a taste of each of these and try to highlight some of the evidence they offer.

The first is the Bible's archaeological accuracy. I have enjoyed reading a lot of archaeology over the years, and especially the works of Dr. William Albright, professor emeritus at Johns Hopkins University. Dr. Albright was a brilliant scholar in his field, but when he moved out of archaeology into prophecy he was horrible. He made statements such as "We can't find the Hittites!" (The Hittites were a large, much-talked-about group of people in the Old Testament.) Albright and his companions said, "Well, where are they? This just proves once again that the Bible is inaccurate." Then some archaeologist would come along and say, "Guess what, I was digging a hole over there in the Middle East and I found the Hittites!" The most embarrassing moment in the life of an archaeologist turned prophet, is when someone digs up what he said didn't exist. (By the way, Albright prophesied in 1948 that the Jews would not go back into their land and become a state.) If he opened his mouth to prophesy, you were sure to win if you chose the opposite opinion. Nevertheless, Albright was a great archaeologist, and after a life of study and excavation in the Middle East he concluded, "There can be no doubt that archaeology has confirmed the substantial historicity of Old Testament tradition." [2]

Albright's conclusion is supported by that of Sir Frederic Kenyon, the former director of the British Museum:

> It is therefore legitimate to say that, in respect of that part of the Old Testament against which the disintegrating criticism of the last half of the nineteenth century was chiefly directed, the evidence of archaeology has been to reestablish its authority and likewise to augment its value by rendering it more intelligible through a fuller knowledge of its background and setting. Archaeology has not yet said its last word, but the results already achieved confirm what faith would suggest—that the Bible can do nothing but gain from an increase in knowledge. [3]

These experts attest to the Bible's archaeological accuracy.

Then there is the matter of its historical accuracy. There was a man by the name of Sir William Ramsay who set out to prove the Bible false by using its historical events and then proving them wrong, especially in the book of Acts. He decided he was going to go everywhere and do everything that Luke recorded about himself, Paul, and the others in the book of Acts, and thereby show that it couldn't be done (for example, taking a boat from one point to another in a certain period of time). He took the same kind of boat that they must have had, left from the same point and journeyed to the same place, trying to see if they could have made it in the recorded period of time. When he completed his study, he not only accepted the Bible as his base, but he made the statement that Luke was probably the most accurate historian of his time:

> Luke is a historian of the first rank; not merely are his statements of fact trustworthy; he is possessed of the true historic sense; he fixed his mind on the idea and plan that rules in the evolution of history, and proportions the scale of his treatment to the importance of each incident. . . . In short, this author should be placed along with the very greatest of historians.[4]

He was overwhelmed with the Bible's historical accuracy.

Now this accuracy does not prove that the Bible is supernatural, but it does indicate that if it is accurate in the details—in the things that don't matter a whole lot—it is more likely to be accurate in the things that do matter a whole lot.

I think it is also important to point out how the biblical documents compare with other ancient documents. Now most ancient documents aren't the type of reading one would typically pick up for an evening's enjoyment. But then again, maybe some of you would. One night I was speaking on this and commented, "Now there's Tacitus, whom some of you probably read last night" (just joking, and everyone laughed). One lady in the front said, "I did, I did!" She was an exception, I'm sure. Tacitus was a Roman historian of the late first and early second centuries. One thousand years later, there were twenty copies of what he wrote. The original had been lost—only twenty copies existed. Caesar's *Gallic Wars* has the same kind of spread. Only eight copies exist today. Thucydides, a Greek writer often cited, is represented by five or six documents after a period of thirteen hundred years.

Now no one is getting really upset about the accuracy of what these writers said. No one is very interested in it, and no one questions it. Kenyon comments, "Scholars are satisfied that they possess substantially the true text of the principal Greek and Roman writers whose works have come down to us, of Sophocles, of Thucydides, of Cicero, of Virgil; yet our knowledge of their writings depends on a mere handful of manuscripts, whereas the manuscripts of the New Testament are counted by hundreds, and even thousands."[5]

Now when we bring the Bible into focus here, and compare it with these other ancient documents, we find it is supported by the strongest evidence possible. Kenyon continues:

It cannot be too strongly asserted that in substance the text of the Bible is certain. Especially is this the case with the New Testament. The number of manuscripts of the New Testament, of early translations from it, and of quotations from it in the oldest writers of the Church, is so large that it is practically certain that the true reading of every doubtful passage is preserved in some one or other of these ancient authorities. This can be said of no other ancient book in the world.[*]

There are thousands of manuscripts of portions of the Bible, some of them written within sixty, fifty, and even forty years of the event.

It's been interesting to watch how scholars keep moving the dates of the Gospels back. They used to say the Gospels were written about A.D. 110. Then they moved it to A.D. 100, A.D. 90, A.D. 80, A.D. 70, and they are still moving it back today. Through more and more historical discoveries, we are finding that the Gospels were written very close to the event. Harold J. Greenlee, professor of New Testament Greek at Oral Roberts University, states, "The earliest extant manuscripts of the New Testament were written much closer to the date of the original writing than is the case in almost any other piece of ancient literature."[7]

In the Old Testament we have a manuscript that is dated A.D. 900. Because that used to be the oldest manuscript of the Old Testament, many have speculated, "Well, if the Old Testament we have is dated A.D. 900, certainly a lot of inaccuracies must have developed in the hundreds of years before, a lot of bad copying and that kind of thing." This kind of speculation leads to some very interesting arguments. As a matter of fact, some Jewish scholars have said that Isaiah 53 (which prophesies that the Messiah will come and suffer for the sins of the world) was written by the Church. "There's no doubt about it, it had to be; it sounds too much like Jesus."

Micah 5:2 says that the Messiah will be born in Bethlehem. Liberal scholars have estimated that Micah was written around 250 B.C., but they are quick to make an exception for that one verse. They don't like that verse, because it talks about the Messiah being born in Bethlehem. That's supernatural! Therefore, it must have been inserted after the event.

Then the Dead Sea Scrolls were found. These Old Testament manuscripts are dated at approximately 150 B.C. All of these scrolls (and they are still being worked on) have proven to be 98.33% exactly the same as documents dated later.[8] "It is a matter of wonder that through something like a thousand years the text underwent so little alteration. As I said in my first article on the scroll, 'Herein lies its chief importance, supporting the fidelity of the Masoretic tradition.'"[9] There were very few inaccuracies, very few changes—it's amazing! Every book in the Old Testament is represented in the discovery of the Dead Sea Scrolls except the book of Esther.

Isaiah 53 is there, and if you can read the Hebrew, you can go to the Shrine of the Scroll in Jerusalem some day and say, "Yes, that's it, that's Isaiah 53, I saw it!" It was not written by the Church, but was in existence for at least two centuries before the Church was founded.

> Of the 166 words in Isaiah 53, there are only seventeen letters in question. Ten of these letters are simply a matter of spelling, which does not affect the sense. Four more letters are minor stylistic changes, such as conjunctions. The remaining three letters comprise the word "light," which is added in verse 11, and does not affect the meaning greatly. . . . Thus, in one chapter of 166 words, there is only one word (three letters) in question after a thousand years of transmission—and this word does not significantly change the meaning of the passage.[10]

Micah 5: 2 was there, too. All the things that had been thrown up as inaccuracies were there, a thousand years before the A.D. 900 manuscript.

I have a friend whose name is Arnold Fruchtenbaum. He's a Hebrew-Christian. Arnold's grandfather was the rabbi of a very, very, very conservative Jewish sect, located in Siberia where he was born. His grandfather knew the Jewish Bible (Old Testament) so well that when a spike was driven through it, he could tell exactly which words it had touched on every page. That's an example of the standard of accuracy with which they copied and transferred the Word of God. They considered it the holy Word of God. They counted the words within a book to make sure they had the exact number, and so many words on each page. They were very, very careful, and they produced a very, very accurate copy of the original.

Prophecy

In my opinion, a lot of bad stuff has come out on prophecy, most of which isn't worth looking into. For instance, some have said that the red dragon in Revelation must mean China. Why is that? You can't reason from what you see around you and then decide what you want a verse to be talking about. When you are trying to find out what a verse in the Bible means, you have to study how it was used within its cultural setting. Some teachers of prophecy say that when Revelation speaks of people mounting up with wings as eagles and fleeing to the mountains it means that Israelis are going to be fleeing their land in United States airplanes (the eagle being a symbol for the U.S.A.). That's ridiculous! Such thinking has no controls. Whatever you think is there is there, and that's foolishness.

There are two things that I believe are very clear in prophecy—Christ's first coming and Christ's second coming. In discussing the first coming I will mention eight specific prophecies that are very simple, but very interesting. When Christ came on the scene, there were two concepts concerning the Messiah: one was that the Messiah was going to come and reign, the other that the Messiah was going to come and die. Now, if you were a Jew, sitting in captivity under the persecution and harassment of the Romans, which Messiah would you like to have come? It was not time for one to die, that's for sure! Although some were still holding to the two-Messiah concept at Christ's coming, there were many who believed just what the Old Testament prophesied. It said He was: 1) to be born in Bethlehem,[11] 2) to be preceded by a messenger,[12] 3) to enter Jerusalem on a donkey,[13] 4) to be betrayed by a friend,[14] 5) to be sold for thirty pieces of silver;[15] 6) this money was to be thrown down in God's house and given for a potters field;[16] 7) he did not retaliate against his accusers;[17] 8) his hands and feet were to be pierced,[18] and he would be crucified with thieves.[19]

Peter Stoner, in a book entitled *Science Speaks,* calculates that the possibility of a person fulfilling all eight of these would be one times ten to the seventeenth power. I'm not much of a mathematician, but I believe that's one with eighteen zeros following it, and those are high odds. Stoner made the analogy: take that many silver dollars, one times ten to the seventeenth power, lay them on the surface of Texas, and they will cover all of the state two feet deep; mark one of them, stir it up with the others, blindfold a man, and he must pick up the marked coin in his first try. One times ten to the seventeenth power. That's very difficult! Now if the number of prophecies was increased from eight to forty-eight (there are about sixty major ones in all), consider the possibility of one person fulfilling all of them. These prophecies don't deal with generalities—such as it will be a depressing day, the economy will have a bad time, there will be clouds this month. They are very specific. The possibility that all forty-eight of these would by chance be true of one man is one times ten to the 157th power. That's a lot of zeros! [20]

One of the prophecies of Christ's first coming that I think is especially outstanding is Daniel 9: 24–27. There it says that 483 years after the decree to rebuild Jerusalem and its walls (given in 445 B.C.) The Messiah, the Prince, will come. I believe that's why many people, as we see in the Gospels, were looking for the Messiah at that time, because it was around A.D. 30 that the Messiah, the Prince, was to come.[21] That's a pretty accurate prophecy written five hundred years before Jesus ever came on the scene.

The second coming is also very interesting. The Bible prophesies in what context the Messiah will come and what state the world is going to be in when he comes to set up his kingdom. In Leviticus 26, Deuteronomy 28, and Deuteronomy 30 we read that although Israel will be scattered throughout the world, she will return to her land and become a nation. The fulfillment of this occurred in 1949. It was also prophesied that she would take over the city of Jerusalem. This didn't happen until 1967, in the Six-day War.

The third thing it says about Israel is that she will rebuild the temple before Jesus comes back to reign. On the sixth day of the Six-day War, when Israel was going in to take the city of Jerusalem, some scrolls were found at the edge of the city. These were called the "Temple Scrolls," and they were written up in *Time, Newsweek,* and so on. The scrolls will be used as instructions to rebuild the Temple on its historic site.

As you may know, this might present a little problem. You can't build a temple on that site until the little building presently there is moved off, and the little building presently on the site belongs to the Arabs. The Mosque of Omar (The Dome of the Rock) is the second most holy spot in the Islamic religion—the religion of the Arab world. One surefire way to get a few Arabs hot is to start knocking down that building! When Hildad, the Israeli historian, was asked, "When are you going to build the temple?" he said, "Well, it will probably take us a generation, just as it did with David when he came back from the land." They replied, "But what about that temple over there, what about that mosque?" He smiled and answered, "Maybe there will be an earthquake, who knows?" Jews who take the Old Testament seriously are talking about the temple. They are even selling temple bonds, if you care to buy them, in Los Angeles or Miami.

There is also a prophecy in Ezekiel 1:38 which states that the King of the North (from the northernmost parts of Israel) will come and set up an alignment of powers with the nations immediately bordering Israel. If you take a line directly north from Israel, you come to the King of the North, which I believe is the Russian government. Whether they will be in the form they are now or not, I don't know. Neither do I know when all this will happen. I'm just trying to help set a possible context here. The Russian people did not go against Israel in an alignment of power with the Arab nations until 1967. They were trying to get Israel without going to war against her, so they armed the Arabs and took the side of the Arab people. It happened just as Ezekiel said it would.

It's also interesting to note that prophecy indicates that the economic center of the world will be moved to the Middle East. In Zechariah 5:5–11 it says that the *ephah,* a Hebrew term used for the commercial center, will be moved to Shinar. Shinar is a Middle East location, and this prophecy indicates that before the Messiah comes back the economic center, the commercial center of the world, will be in Shinar. Who would have thought a few years ago that this Middle East oil mess would so radically alter world economics right now, in this time, in our day? Things seem to be falling into place for the Messiah to come back. I don't think it's wise to talk about time, but I do think it's interesting to see that world events are occurring just as the Bible said they would.

The ecological problems we are facing today are also talked

about in the Bible. A lot of people say, "Hey, wait a minute, you can't talk about wars and rumors of wars and famines and earthquakes as being a fulfillment of prophecy. There have always been wars and rumors of wars, there have always been famines, there have always been earthquakes!" That's true, but when Christ talks about these he speaks of them as birth pangs, and he says that there will be more and more of them, and they will be more intensive. It's like the intensity of pain a woman experiences while giving birth to a child. The birth pangs occur more frequently and become more intense until finally she gives birth. That's the image that Christ is trying to present. Unity, accuracy, prophecy—both of the first and second coming.

Claims of Jesus

The fourth reason why I believe the Bible is a supernatural revelation from God is the claim to deity that Jesus made. He came saying this—"I am the God-Man." He said it in many ways. "If you've heard Me, you've heard God." [22] "If you've seen Me, you've seen God." [23] "If you know Me, you know God." [24] "If you've received Me, you've received God." [25] "If you've honored Me, you've honored God." [26] He was trying to get a point across—he was claiming to be equal to God. The chief priest walked up to him in John 8 and said, "Are you the one who claims to be the Messiah, from the Old Testament?" And he said, "Yes, that's me." Many liberal scholars would say he didn't mean that. He meant something "deeper." It's like if I were to see an old acquaintance and say, "Bob, are you the same Bob Lowden that I remember attending a seminar with a few years ago?" And he said, "Yeah, that's me." And I said, "Ah, really, you don't mean that, do you? You mean something 'deeper.'" No! He meant what he said—he's Bob Lowden. Jesus said exactly what he meant when he said he was the Messiah. "A man who can read the New Testament and not see that Christ claims to be more than a man, can look all over the sky at high noon on a cloudless day and not see the sun." [27]

C. S. Lewis, one of the greatest scholars of our century, argues it this way. The claim of Jesus that he was the God-Man is either true or false. If it's true, Jesus is the God-Man. If it's false, either he knew it was false, or he didn't know it was false. If he knew it was false—he really knew he wasn't the God-Man—but he was running around anyway saying, "I am the God-Man," what was He doing? Lying—he was an imposter! On the other hand, if he didn't know it was false—he thought he was the God-Man, but really wasn't—and he was running around saying, "I am the God-Man," what was he? He was nuts! That's it; those are the only alternatives we have. He was either lying, he was mentally unbalanced, or He actually was the God-Man. [28]

I AM THE GOD-MAN

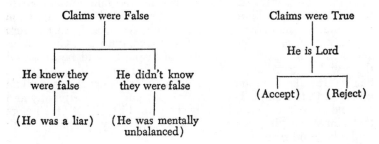

Some people try to draw a line right down the center of this and say, "He was an outstanding teacher, the most exemplary person in the history of mankind. He would have made 'Who's Who in Jerusalem' if he had stuck around long enough. Too bad he died." But wait a minute, He didn't leave that alternative open to us. Either he was a liar, or he was mentally unbalanced, or he was the God-Man. Period.

Passing Jesus off as an outstanding teacher or a great example after hearing his claims would be synonymous to passing me off as a "great guy" after hearing me claim I was a poached egg. Imagine for a moment that I am not Tim Timmons, and I tell you, "Hey, I'm not Tim Timmons, I'm a poached egg." (Some of you may think, "Um, could be!") Now you would have to take me through the same kind of grid. I am either lying, mentally unbalanced, or I really am, I truly am, the first poached egg you have ever seen walk or talk. I guarantee though, after a very short time of my telling you that I am a poached egg, and you see that I really do believe I am a poached egg, you will not say, "You know, even though he claims to be a poached egg, he's a 'great guy.'" You don't do that with people like that. You get help for them!

Napoleon Bonaparte said, "I know men and I tell you that Jesus Christ is no mere man. Between him and every other person in the world there is no possible term of comparison. Alexander, Caesar, Charlemagne and I have founded empires. But on what did we rest the creations of our genius? Upon force. Jesus Christ founded his empire upon love; and at this hour millions of men would die for him." [29]

Jesus claimed to be the God-Man, and that claim is the best indication, the greatest proof, that there is something unusual about the Bible. He claimed that he was speaking from the Bible and that what he was saying was authoritatively coming from God. Many have claimed to be prophets or messengers from God. Jesus of Nazareth claimed to be God. He is the only man who has ever come along saying that he was the God-Man, and every one of us has to decide what to do with his claims.

The evidence at this point is the discovery of a supernatural revelation from God to man. This supernatural revelation of God (both the written Word and the living Word) lays a foundation for me to relate confidently to the supernatural God of the universe.

THE SUPERNATURAL RELATIONSHIP

It has been said, "The heart cannot delight in what the mind cannot accept." Because people continually ignore that principle, many have emotionally accepted or rejected Christianity without really understanding it. As Arnold Toynbee observed, "People have not rejected Christianity, but a poor caricature of it." The biblical revelation is not just another book of pious platitudes and religious rhetoric. It's a supernatural revelation that explains life as it is and people as they are. Built upon this crucial foundation is the reality of the supernatural relationship.

The Plan

According to the supernatural revelation, the original plan was for man to enjoy a relationship with God. It was through this relationship that man was to know and experience total fulfillment and full expression of himself as a human being. This relationship was intended to give man a reference point from which to enjoy life through relating properly to other people and to the entire creation.

The Problem

The plan was beautiful, but man botched it royally. As the bumper sticker says, "If you feel far from God, who moved?" Man finds himself separated from God and his plan because of his own self-centered rebellion.

Man has an optical problem—the big "I." "The world must revolve around me. God, you go your way, I'll go mine. Check with me when I'm seventy-one or seventy-two and we'll negotiate!" Man continues to wreck his life by rebelling against God's master plan of life, trying to run it on his own. Whether he experiences a personal crisis or an inner hollowness, his life is unsatisfying because he's not experiencing the maximum life for which he was created. The tragedy is that the effects of the wreckage of one's life are not limited to himself. It affects those around him as well. Without the supernatural, vertical relationship as a foundation, most horizontal relationships seem to disintegrate.

We have a desperate problem. We are separated from the God of the universe by our rebellion—our sin. It's like being separated by a great canyon that no one is able to cross on his own, even though we make many admirable attempts. Some try by living a good life. Some give to charities. Many become religious. Others try the intellectual route. Still no one is able to cross the canyon to the other side. It's humanly impossible!

Let's suppose that you and I are walking along the edge of a forty-foot canyon, and we want to get across to the other side. You suggest, "Let's jump!" I say, "O.K., but you go first!" So you back up about fifty yards and run like crazy toward the edge. As you spring from your side you push off with every ounce of strength you can muster. It's a noble jump—thirty-five feet, eleven inches. After I see you jump, I back up about ten yards and run toward the edge, giving it all I've got—ten feet, five and one-half inches. As you are soaring through the air in front of me, you glance back and think how much better you're doing than I. However, in a few seconds, we are both lying at the bottom of the canyon in critical condition. Why? People can't jump forty-foot canyons—they need a bridge.

The Payment

To put man's problem in another way, man is in debt to God. For our self-centered rebellion (our sin) God requires a payment. One of the most natural instincts of man is to try to pay for his own guilt. Man feels he must pay for what he does wrong and for his shortcomings. Everyone attempts to pay in different ways. Some pay by being down on themselves, even to the point of depression. Others pay by depriving themselves of something. An increasing number are attempting to make the ultimate payment by killing themselves, but none of these self-imposed payments really satisfies. The debt remains—man is guilty before God.

Counseling rooms are filled with people who are guilt ridden, seeking for a payment that will give them the confidence that the debt is paid. Professional counselors offer three possible payments. First is the transfer method: "Blame it on someone else, something else, any person or any thing. Blame it on the environment, blame it on society." "It's a wonder that anyone comes out healthy, living in such a sick society." "Blame it on your parents or your mate. Whatever you do, transfer the blame away from yourself." This will relieve your sense of responsibility in the situation so that you cannot be held responsible. (Of course, you only want to apply this to the bad or wrong that you do; you want personal credit for the good!) It's true that we are all greatly affected by other people and circumstances, but a person must accept responsibility for his own actions. If he doesn't, who will?

The second method of dealing with guilt is to lower or do away with the standard or principle that was broken. "Who makes up the rules anyway?" If a person breaks the marital bond through an extramarital affair, then let's lighten the importance of the marital bond. Take this approach to its logical end and you create a society in which everyone does whatever he decides is right. It seems this is one of the most popular themes today—"Do your own thing!" (Sometimes known as, "If it feels good, do it!") The progression in this kind of reasoning is: 1) It all depends on how you look at it; 2) it really doesn't matter how you look at it, and finally; 3) I don't think anybody knows how to look at it. Therefore, do your own thing! The result—chaos!

The third method used to deal with guilt is escape. "Move!" Where? How about central Africa? Escape—to any place you are unknown and cannot be pressured or reminded of your particular crisis situation. Without a doubt, "getting away" for a time may be helpful. But you cannot continue to run. In order to be freed from the guilt connected with a particular problem, you must face it head on. Otherwise, it will never go away, but will hide in the subconscious waiting to haunt you.

All three methods of dealing with personal guilt are not really payments of the debt at all. They are simply methods by which we ignore the problem, hoping to alleviate the "guilties." Some people find temporary relief this way, only to despair later as the cancerous beast once again raises its ugly head. Many walk away from the counseling room in despair, because they are still weighted down with the guilt and have been given no hope of relief.

There are only two ways to pay for what you have done wrong (your sin—the self-centered rebellion that separates you from God). 1) You can pay for it by dying for eternity—that's a long time and hardly a possible payment. 2) You can accept God's payment of Jesus Christ's death on the cross. You see, Jesus, the God-Man, didn't come to set up another religious system, but by his death to make a payment for your sin so that you need not pay anymore. The death of the God-Man is the only payment that is adequate to pay for all of mankind's sins.

The Payoff

Let's go back to our mythical forty-foot canyon again (after recovering from our jump). Since we cannot jump it, we must find a bridge. According to the biblical base Jesus of Nazareth, the God-Man, is the only one who can span the forty feet. He has bridged the great gap between God and man. Let's say that we just admire the bridge and discuss how truly remarkable it is. Nothing happens! There is no supernatural transference from one side to the other without actually getting on the bridge.

We must cross over that bridge. Realizing that we cannot make an adequate payment for the sin that separates us from God, and that the only adequate payment is the death of Christ (the God-Man), we must receive his payment on our behalf. That's getting on the bridge—personally counting on and receiving God's payment for our sin. It's as if a pardon were offered to a criminal on death row. He can accept it or reject it, but it will not affect his life unless he actually receives it for himself. When we receive God's payment for sin, the payoff is made.

The evidence that a person has entered into the supernatural relationship is a gut-level feeling of peace. This is the peace that comes from having your guilt paid for. This is the peace that comes from knowing that you're not all alone in the universe. This is the peace that comes from looking through the new "glasses" God has given you which help you see that life is not out of control, but is in the hands of a personal God who cares. This is a deep inner peace.

Another element of evidence related to peace within us is love for others. Through the supernatural revelation we are given a basis for loving people unconditionally—God's love for us. The spiritual relationship with God gives us a new capacity to love people unconditionally.

Still another evidence of the supernatural relationship is an inner sense of destiny. This sense of destiny promises meaningfulness (abundance) in this life and heaven in the life to come. In a word, this sense of destiny gives us hope to go on living.

None of these pieces of criminal evidence can be experienced perfectly. Christianity is not synonymous with perfection. There is freedom to fail and it is a fact that we will all fail at times.

The ultimate life style does not guarantee that one who lives it will always be on top of the pile. The piles will be encountered and the believer may have to go under them, around them, or even shovel through them. There may often be stress instead of peace, resentment and self-centeredness instead of unconditional love, and a sense of hopelessness instead of hope. The difference is that these times of stress, self-centeredness, and hopelessness can be relieved when the believer returns to his base—the supernatural revelation from God. Because God is really there and cares, we can be encouraged and recharged to get back up when we fall down.

The supernatural relationship built upon the supernatural revelation heightens my personal confidence in the supernatural God.

If you can find a better base—by all means, buy it!

FOOTNOTES
for Appendix A

1. Clark H. Pinnock, *Set Forth Your Case* (Chicago: Moody, 1967), p. 124.
2. W. F. Albright, *Archaeology and the Religion of Israel* (Baltimore: Johns Hopkins, 1942), p. 176.
3. Sir Frederic Kenyon, *The Bible and Archaeology* (New York: Harper & Brothers, 1940), p. 279.
4. Sir W. M. Ramsay, *The Bearing of Recent Discovery on the Trustworthiness of the the New Testament* (London: Hodder and Stoughton, 1915), p. 222.
5. Sir Frederic Kenyon, *Our Bible and the Ancient Manuscripts* (New York: Harper & Brothers, 1941), p. 23.
6. Ibid., p. 23.
7. J. Harold Greenlee, *Introduction to New Testament Textual Criticism* (Grand Rapids: Eerdmans, 1964), p. 15.
8. Norman L. Geisler and William E. Nix, *A General Introduction to the Bible* (Chicago: Moody, 1968), p. 365.
9. Ibid., p. 261.
10. Ibid., p. 263.
11. Prophecy: Micah 5: 2, Fulfillment: Matthew 2: 1.
12. Prophecy: Isaiah 40: 3, Fulfillment: Matthew 3: 1-2.
13. Prophecy: Zechariah 9: 9, Fulfillment: Luke 19: 35-37a.
14. Prophecy: Psalm 41: 9, Fulfillment: Matthew 10: 4.
15. Prophecy: Zechariah 11: 12, Fulfillment: Matthew 26: 15.
16. Prophecy: Zechariah 11: 13b, Fulfillment: Matthew 27: 5a.
17. Prophecy: Isaiah 53: 7, Fulfillment: Matthew 27: 12-19.
18. Prophecy: Psalm 22:16, Fulfillment: Luke 23: 33.
19. Prophecy: Isaiah 53: 12, Fulfillment: Matthew 27: 38.
20. Peter W. Stoner, *Science Speaks* (Chicago: Moody, 1963), pp. 100–107.
21. Robert Anderson, *The Coming Prince* (Grand Rapids: Kregel), p. 127.
22. John 14: 10.
23. John 14: 9.
24. John 8: 19.
25. Mark 9: 37.
26. John 5: 23.
27. Frank Mead (ed.), *The Encyclopedia of Religious Quotations* (Westwood: Fleming H. Revell, n.d.), p. 50.
28. C. S. Lewis, *Mere Christianity* (New York: MacMillan, 1943), p. 56.
29. Mead, op. cit., p. 56.